The Undead Bonds

OrangeBooks Publication

Smriti Nagar, Bhilai, Chhattisgarh - 490020

Website: **www.orangebooks.in**

© Copyright, 2023, Author

All rights reserved. No part of this book may be reproduced, stored in a retrieval system, or transmitted, in any form by any means, electronic, mechanical, magnetic, optical, chemical, manual, photocopying, recording or otherwise, without the prior written consent of its writer.

THE UNDEAD BONDS

A Father-Daughter Story in a Post-apocalyptic World

BHARGAV MEHTA

OrangeBooks Publication
www.orangebooks.in

They act how they feel
The feed how they want,
The prophecy of the humans,
The kingdom of theirs hearts,

They all turn

ACKNOWLEDGEMENTS

I owe a big debt of gratitude to my wonderful parents, Sachin and Tanvi Mehta, for everything they have done for me.

And a big thank you to all the wonderful individuals who encouraged me to create this magnum opus fiction come to life through this novel; I had the pleasure of meeting these amazing friends who have since become my best friends, including: Atharva Kulthe, Arya Manek, Arya Thacker, Arsh Memon, Yash Bhansari, along with other amazing friends throughout this journey.

Finally, thank you to everyone who was left out; you all made my life wonderful.

CONTENT

ONE
Is The Dinner Ready? 1

TWO
The Interview 7

THREE
The Virus 14

FOUR
7 Years Later 36

FIVE
The Gas Station 63

SIX
The Nine Floors Of Death 73

SEVEN
THE EXECUTION 110

EIGHT
THE GORDIAN KNOT 142

NINE
MORIBUND 158

TEN
THE LEVEL FIVE 172

ELEVEN
THE FINAL WAR 180

TWELVE
DEAD BUT ALIVE 192

ONE

Is The Dinner Ready?

"Hello! Hello! Is this Mr. John from the medical department I'm speaking with?" said the lady on the phone

"You are, indeed. "How may I help you?" John responded.

It was a late frigid night, everyone was asleep, while it was snowing outside. "Sir, we were curious about the virus." stated the lady

"I'm at a loss for words."

"But, Sir, people are dying at the hands of you." Before John hung up the phone, the lady added

24 hours earlier

Year 2024, at John's house, they were having a family dinner. Sally asked her brother, "hand me the salt!" in a gruff tone. "Hey! Watch your tone." John stated as Sally said "Yeah," with a slight chuckle. "Mike, would you mind turning on the TV for me?" John asked.

"Yeah, sure thing." Mike replied while standing up to fetch the remote. "Bring me a glass of water, Mike." Sally stated as she attempted to annoy Mike once again.

"NOOOO, go get it yourself." Mike responded in an angry and frustrated voice. "How could you be so weak?" Sally made a point of saying sarcastically "I'm better than you!"

"SHUT UP, YOU TWO! Go to your room RIGHT NOW!" As he began to lose his mind, John yelled angrily, Mike and Sally both walked to their room. On this late night, John was stressed and even though he had been contemplating an issue that had rendered his life difficult, he carefully strolled from the dining hall to his couch and began watching the news. All of the news networks were presenting the same viral information. Something previously unseen or unheard of has been found through science. After learning about the disease, John immediately began reading the news. He was paying attention since he worked in a laboratory that had discovered this specific virus. The reporter stated that there is no need for humans to fear a virus that has only been observed in ants.

This virus is highly lethal for ants as it causes them to lose control of their cognitive functions and engage in cannibalistic behaviour. However, humans doesn't need to be concerned about contracting this virus as we all possess robust immune systems that make it impossible for us to be affected by such a pathogen. As the news came to an end, John stood up and expressed his need for rest. It was already eleven o'clock, and he had work the next day. He began to walk towards his room when he noticed that Sally was still awake, watching videos in bed. John approached her door and knocked. Sally promptly opened the door, seemingly irritated and asked, "What do you want?" in a raised tone.

"You should sleep since you have school in the morning." John stated as Sally slammed the door behind her, making an irritating noise. John was disappointed, but he still left to check on Mike. He was about to go to bed when he saw John and addressed him as "Dad." And asked "What were they discussing in the news, Dad?".

"Nothing," John sighed, "it was just a new virus discovered by science, nothing to worry about."

"OK". Mike replied with a soft smile on his face. "Now go to bed since you have school tomorrow," John said as he began to make his way towards his bedroom. Mike returned his gaze and slowly dropped his light before retiring to bed.

Time flew by.

Mike and John got up early as normal and started prepping. Mike walked inside Sally's room, only to find her missing. In awe, Mike shouted, "DAD!"

"What happened"? As he went to Mike with dishes in his hand, John remarked, "Why are you screaming?" Sally asked as she walked out of the shower. "Never mind dad, I found her." Mike stated as he took a moment to breathe. "More like I found you". Sally Responded, John dashed into Sally's room and exclaimed, "You woke up early? In those other words, how did this miracle happen? Anyway, I have to get going. You both get ready and leave as soon as possible." John turned and walked away. Sally and Mike began to prepare for their day at school. Sally was a brilliant girl, but she was uninterested in everything. They both hopped on their bikes, and Mike found his friends along the way while Sally, on the other hand, was waiting for her friends. She waited about thirty minutes, but no one showed up, causing her to be late for school.

"Why were you late yet again?" her teacher grew frustrated. Your brother came before you, and this isn't the first time you've been late." The teacher said

"Next time, I'll be more careful," Sally remarked as the teacher appeared tired of having Sally grasp the same subject repeatedly. "May I please have a seat now?" Sally inquired as the teacher became progressively furious.

"Today, despite our many conversations, you will not sit in my class." The teacher responded while Sally began to apologize to her, saying, "It won't happen again, kindly give me another chance." The teacher didn't care at this point. She had made her final choice.

Mike raised his hand as he watched his sister standing. "Ma'am, can I take the punishment instead of Sally?" he asked the teacher. The teacher was perplexed but also delighted to see Mike standing up for his sister. "Why would you, Mike? Sally made a mistake, so she only has to accept the punishment," the teacher said.

Time passed and the lessons continued till it was the end of the school day as everyone rushed out of the classroom to go home. The teacher observed Sally packing her bag and approached her. "Sally, I apologize if you felt insulted; my intentions were not to hurt you, but to try and make you a better person; I hope to see some changes in you after today; it will be good for you." Sally tentatively exited the classroom and went outside, where she discovered every one of her friends leaving without calling or waiting for her. She walked to her bike, unhappy when she discovered that everyone had left and that only Mike was waiting for her solitary. He accompanied Sally on her way back home as He felt bad for his sister, so he tried to convince her that she should work on her anger and stop being rude to others, which would help her in the future. "Why aren't you with your friends?" Sally spoke up.

"I'm trying to help you; I want you to understand that being rude will not help you in the future, just as your friends will not join you because of your rudeness." Mike stated. He didn't like how Sally spoke to him, so he accelerated his bike and tried to catch back to his friends.

Sally continued her journey alone

Mike was chatting about his sister in front of his classmates when he unexpectedly ground to a halt. When his buddies tried to reach Mike, he turned his bike around and began riding on the other side of his friends. Mike took a shortcut to his house as He appeared to be in a rush. He was going through the motions until he noticed something.

He noticed a path through the woods that was very long but shorter than his usual route home, so Mike decided to take this route home. The path had become entirely overrun with huge and small trees, along with a variety of flora. It was also a bit tough to look though due to all the barriers in the Centre. "I should probably hurry up". Mike said as he continued on his journey, fog began to form and cover the entire area, making it difficult for him to see. Mike continued on his way, unconcerned about how bad the situation was around him. He was caught in a situation where he couldn't see the path after a few minutes of continuous cycling. He was tired and dehydrated, He had the sensation that something was happening to him that he had never felt before.

His brain shut down; he lost track of what he was doing, where he was going, and where he was. In no time, he was knocked out. It felt like a dream. He was genuinely bewildered.

He saw the entire city running around the streets, people burning their own houses, and people fleeing from other people. "Where am I?" he wondered. What's going on? "Why are they running?" He was so perplexed that he approached one of those people and attempted to question them about what was going on, but instead of answering, one of them ran towards him and attempted to kill him. He awoke immediately and hoped on his bike, attempting to find his way back home. "What is going on?" What was that? "Why were people escaping from each other, and why did that guy attack me?" Mike stated while He was failing to find his way back. "What's going on, I- I can't"? Mike said as He tried different paths, but surprisingly ended up back where he began. This continued for several minutes until he could finally hear the vehicles. He quickly turned his bike around and started riding in the direction. "Come on, a little bit more." Mike said

He eventually saw the road and pedalled as quickly as he could to get home. After a few minutes, he returned home.

TWO

The Interview

Mike turned the television on instantly after reaching home. He grabbed some food and turned on the news. It was his dad who was about to be interviewed today. Sally had never seen her father on television, despite the fact that he was a brilliant scientist who appeared on numerous news channels and interviews. "Good morning, today I am with a well-known scientist, Mr. John Baker "How are you, sir?" The interviewer inquired.

"I'm feeling great, Thank you." Said John

"Wonderful, Sir, so what are you currently researching on?" The interviewer inquired as John stated that "We're currently focused on this virus, which only affects ants, as we saw in the news yesterday, and to see if there's any chance it could affect humans, which would be extremely dangerous. It has the potential to cause chaos in this city, which could occur".

"Do you mean it has the potential to affect humans? Because we didn't hear anything about it "... According to the interviewer

"Yes, we can't just say it won't have an effect without doing research on it; even small insects can be dangerous to humans in other ways. It's impossible to say whether it's safe for us without proper research" John stated

"So, you're saying the news was incorrect?" The interviewer inquired

"It's impossible to say that without proper observation." John stated

"That was a little frightening to hear, but thank you so much for getting involved in today's interview. And we very much hope to see you again someday." From the interviewer. John was a little perplexed, but he shook hands with the interviewer and stepped up. John left the interview area and headed again to his lab to start his research. He was worried about the virus's impact on humans. Other scientists soon entered his lab and started to conflict over the virus. "Do you really believe it will have an effect on the human world?" According to one scientist.

"What you said in the interview terrified the entire city. John, are you aware of this?" The second scientist stated

"You are all excellent scientists. You must all be aware of all possibilities." John stated

"We get it, creating fear in humans with your worst-case scenarios." According to one scientist.

"There was nothing wrong with people knowing about this. Tell me, why did you broadcast the virus's news without even properly inspecting it and stating to everyone that it isn't harmful?" John stated

"Okay, John, we've all decided that you won't be researching this virus; we just want you to get out of here." One scientist stated. "You've got to be kidding me," John said, as he was taken aback. "I mean, how can you?"

"GET OUT, JOHN." Scientists stated

With a deep breath, John stood and exited his laboratory. For the first time in his life, he was completely dissatisfied with his teammates. John started his car and drove home with all his thoughts,

He switched on the radio.

He changed stations on the radio numerous times before settling on one that was airing his interview.

"As we all heard in the interview, we can all agree that this thing was a little too frightening for all of us, but I believe it is all a lie. They're getting paid to get interviewed, and then they'll just pretend it was all a ruse and nothing happened". According to the radio host

John became furious. He quickly turned off the radio and continued driving, yet he couldn't stop thinking about the radio and his crew mates, who were accusing him of putting false belief in people, At this point, John tried to remain calm and continued driving. After a few miles, John stooped near a bar to freshen his mood, but it wasn't enough. The people in the bar noticed him and began gossiping about him spreading false information.

John wasn't concerned initially, he sat there contemplating his thoughts when he was approached by a man in a black suit, who was entirely clad in black and appeared to be an agent. He sat alongside John and ordered an alcoholic beverage, then inquired whether he wanted anything, to which John replied, "Nah, I'm fine." The guy wasn't bothered and asked for one scotch for John, who questioned who he was. The individual didn't say anything at first, but after a little conversation, he said, "I can't say." John got frustrated yet again, but he responded calmly, "Why are you here?"

"I'm here to talk about Daisy," the man said.

Upon hearing the name "Daisy," John sprang up in anguish and threw the glass on the seat.

To John's amazement, there was no one in the seat; he was hallucinating, however, the bartender immediately booted him out.

John left the bar.

"They should have let others get interviewed instead of me, no John, you were right, don't think negatively," he said as he got into his car. John began to accelerate his car, and as he drove, he decided to switch on the radio, but this time he chose to listen to music instead of the local stations. He was driving at a constant pace when he got struck from behind by a vehicle. John wasn't seriously harmed, but he was enraged by what had happened to him, and he was essentially out of control at this point. Enraged, John jumped out of his car and began ranting at the individual who had hit his vehicle. "Hey you!" Is this your first time behind the wheel? Are you blind?" John stated.

The person who crashed John's car started to argue with him, and both John and the individual became frustrated. They continued to quarrel until everyone came. They sought to put an end to the argument, which was finally resolved. On his way home, John observed that the entire road seemed deserted, despite the fact that it was the busiest one and regularly occupied with cars and bikes,

However, he didn't think much of it and continued until it commenced to get foggy, the road became engulfed in fog in no time and it became challenging for John to see, John tried to drive his car slow until he could see the road clearly. He kept driving, but since it was still foggy, he pulled over. He got a phone call as he came to a complete halt. When he answered the phone, it was Mike on the other line. He phoned to check on him, and John assured him that he was OK and didn't need to worry. At the same time, John observed a girl and a young boy in the Centre of the foggy road and found it difficult to see them. John merely informed Mike that he was on his way home and hung up the phone. He got out of the car and hurried to them since the road was hazy and the children can get seriously injured. "What are you doing here, and how did you find your way here?" John inquired.

John kept asking them how they got here, but they never responded. John was puzzled, but he was astounded when he noticed that the children were not even looking at him. They didn't move at all. John was merely standing there. He tried to touch them, but when he did, they vanished into thin air. He was completely perplexed at this point. He dashed back to his car, convinced that he was witnessing a nightmare.

John was stressed about a lot of things at the same time at this point, He was still holding up, but after a few minutes of moving, he passed out.

Mike and Sally both watched the interview. Mike felt bad for his father after watching, whereas Sally rushed into her room. When Mike noticed Sally, he decided to pursue her. Sally burst into tears.

The doorbell rang

Mike heard the doorbell and informed Sally that he would be right back for her. He ran to the door and flung it open, only to discover his friends waiting outside.

"Hey guys, this isn't the right time," Mike warned his friends, who seemed to be in a rush. "Mike No, your father has been in an accident just over the street, hurry." As he hurriedly seized his bike and asked Mike to follow, he stated. Mike looked around Sally's room and decided that telling her wasn't a smart idea since she was already worried and he knew it would make her much worse. As they were going, Mike noticed a car on the side of the road that he recognized. "HEYY!" Everyone comes to a complete standstill. Mike noticed John lying inside the car as he approached it. "Dad! Dad! Wake up". Mike said

When John awoke, he was mystified but relieved to see Mike. "Hey, Mike, what's going on? Where am I?" John inquired.

"We found you laying on the ground while we were looking for you," Mike explained.

"Oh my God, I am delighted to see you," John said "Where's Sally?"

"She's at home". Mike replied "But, what were you doing?"

"I'll tell you after we get home," John said as he got in his car, where Mike took his bike and followed him. Although John was in good health and was not in pain, he was still plagued by an unnoticed headache as he returned home. For John, the agony was an absolute catastrophe and it looked like he was doing all he could to escape and forget the pain, which was not helping. They eventually made it home, and as soon as they entered, John fainted once more. "Dad! Dad! "Are you OK?" Mike asked as John remained deafeningly silent. As a result, Mike dialled an ambulance. Sally, on the other hand, attempted to add some water but received no response from John.

After about 20 minutes, an ambulance arrived, grabbed John, and took him with them. Mike grabbed Sally and pulled her to bed, telling her, "You should stay, and I'll go with dad." Sally disagreed with him and told him that they should both stay together. They eventually opted to stay at home together. Following several minutes, Mike spotted Sally weeping in her room. Upon knocking on Sally's door, he headed inside to console her. Mike, as a brother, attempted to cheer her up and prevent her tears with assuring her that Dad would be well and that she should relax till he recovered.

THREE

The Virus

Sally felt relaxed with Mike and was relieved to have him by her side.

The doorbell rang again.

Mike dashed up to the front door to see who was there. He discovered that there was someone wearing a white shirt and a black court on their doorstep. Mike recognized that person and opened the door. The man outside Mike's house was one of the best researchers in his father's laboratory, and there were other scientists knocking on his door as well. Mike greeted them all who were present. "Hello, Mike. I'm Dr Ruthven Ragan, and I'm here to speak with you about your father ".

Dr Ruthven Ragan was a lab researcher who always kept his appearance simple yet professional, often seen wearing a classic white lab coat over a button-up shirt and khaki pants with practical and comfortable shoes, his short hair combed neatly to one side.

"Is he okay?" Mike inquired with an anxious tone.

"We can't say anything, but the real reason we're here is to have you". Ruthven Ragan said

"Why do you need me?" Mike inquired, perplexed.

"We don't have to answer that right now," Ruthven Ragan stated. "Does anyone else live in this house?"

Mike responded "NO" without trepidation, knowing that keeping Sally out of this would be the best thing to do. Mike had no understanding what was going on and had plenty of questions. Sally's condition remained uncertain. Mike was accompanied by Ruthven Ragan, but Sally was still absent. Mike was compelled to enter the car without speaking. He sat in the rear of the car with Dr Ruthven Ragan. "Did your father ever mention anything about an ant virus, Mike?" Dr Ruthven Ragan inquired. Mike remained silent and gazed into the distance. Dr Ruthven Ragan was displeased, but he remained silent with a small smile on his face. The car came to a stop after a sharp turn, and Dr Ruthven Ragan moved for Mike to exit. Mike became aware and obeyed Dr Ruthven Ragan's command. He noticed that they had come to a halt right outside his father's laboratory. He began moving forward and was astonished when he noticed a large door in front of him with no handles.

"Welcome Dr Ruthven Ragan"

Dr Ruthven Ragan's face was recognized, and the laboratory door opened. Mike was trailing him, surrounded by three other scientists. Mike was then escorted to an elevator with the guards. The lift was lowered into the basement. When the door swung open, Mike was taken aback when he saw hundreds of convicts in the enormous high-tech cells. Mike wasn't sure what was going on; however, he had a nasty feeling about it. The guards opened the cell door and ordered him to enter. It was a small cell with no high-tech equipment, and one could even barely fit. There was a small glass attached to the door that allowed user to see outside. Mike was considering various things until he heard loud, disturbing noises.

He looked out the window to see what was going on. A man was attempting to escape from his cell.

He was covered in various substances and was banging toilsome on the cell glass. Mike kept an eye on that man, pleading for his life, but the man was later killed for an unknown reason. Mike sat down and took his hand off the glass, trying to process everything that was going through his mind. Mike was terrified at this point after witnessing the death of a person in the same type of cell as him. All of the cells had been consumed by people, and they were all under high security, except for Mike, who was simply placed in a small regular cell.

Suddenly an alarm went off. When Dr Ruthven heard the alarm, he immediately ordered everyone to leave the laboratory.

Everyone started running, leaving their work undone. This made every cell vulnerable and eventually caused them to break off. Mike was the only one in a small cell, so no one noticed him, but the prisoners were attacking everyone else in that facility. Mike witnessed everyone being attacked and pleading for their lives. They couldn't even walk as they stared at each other. They were out of control and didn't appear to be normal human beings.

15 Minutes earlier.

Dr Ruthven Ragan was already preparing something before the alarm went off. "Access granted; welcome

Dr Ruthven Ragan"

"Sir, we have brought him here exactly as you requested. What comes next?"

"Move aside, let me see." He entered the room and found someone he was eager to meet. "It's fascinating, isn't it? It's John Baker. The only person who was aware of the virus." John was restrained by hard ropes to a chair, unable to move. "What do you want, Ruthen?" John replied

"First and foremost, my name is Ruthven, and secondly, we need your help." Said Dr Ruthven.

"Yeah, go to hell," John answered, his face covered in blood, as if he had been struck in the face while being handcuffed.

"Be careful with your words, because what you say and do affects your son." Dr Ruthven made clear "You don't want anything to happen to your son Mike," "What exactly did you do to him? Reply! "Right now!" John yelled angrily, attempting to shake himself free.

"Don't worry, he's safe and secure with us." We will not harm him unless you don't follow our instructions. "Listen to me, John; you don't have much of a choice; just do what I say, and we'll let you and your son go; it's as simple as that." Ruthven Ragan said

"What should I do?" John inquired.

"Oh, now we're talking," said Dr Ruthven

"As we all know, you're aware of this ant virus, don't you?" Ruthven Ragan said

"Yes". John responded

"Pay very close attention when I'm speaking. Do you have any recollection of the interview, John? As you mentioned, the virus has the potential to infect a human body." Ruthven Ragan said.

"Yeah, but getting infected will take a long time," John replied......

"Well, that's not the case John, The virus is in fact spreading to humans, leaving the bodies of ants and affecting humans." Ruthven Ragan said...

"How are you so sure about that? That's impossible," John replied....

"Let me show you." Ruthven Ragan said

Dr Ruthven took John to the same laboratory where Mike was placed in the cell, he showed John all of the infected bodies that were kept in the cell...

"What are they?" John asked....

"They are infected, what happened was we tried to see if the infection could spread in human bodies, well it does indeed, the problem is we don't have any information about the cure or we aren't even sure what kind of virus this is," Ruthven Ragan said...

"This is dangerous! How many people have you taken for the test?" John asked....

"We only took three people, but the infection was stronger than we expected, it started spreading, It wasn't first tested here but at a different place, before your interview we started to examine the ant's body and the human body, but as I said it went out of control, the whole lab was infected in no time, All the infected were sent here for research, Since you know about the virus we want you to look into it." Ruthven Ragan said.

"How many cells are there?" John asked.

"Well, there are fifty people who are currently infected," Dr Ruthven stated "Let me show you some of the infected people."....

John was caught off guard by the fact that they tried testing the virus on humans before possibly becoming acquainted with the virus as well as attempting to develop a cure, and the most unexpected question he found that he asked Ruthven was that if they witnessed that the first person was successfully infected,

Why didn't they try to find a cure rather than experimenting with on more and more people and even after that when the infection propagated, He inquired whether this was all premeditated before seeking to kill humanity. Ruthven was taken away; he explained that it was a mistake and shifted the subject.

He began showing John some samples of the effects of ants on humans if bitten by an ant. For a brief moment, John couldn't believe what he was seeing. They kept moving and looking at other cells that held the infected. The first cell was made of glass, and the person inside resembled a human but was in poor health. The individual attempted to attack the humans but was stopped by the glass....

"This guy was bitten by a red ant, which turned him into a walking corpse. Just wait until you see the others "said the doctor......

"A walking corpse?"....

"Yes, let me tell you how the infection works. The mechanics of how the infection takes hold can vary, but it's often depicted as a virus or pathogen that takes over the victim's body and reanimates it, turning it into an infected. Once someone is infected, the virus or pathogen is thought to take over their brain and cause them to lose all higher cognitive functions and become a mindless, aggressive creature that seeks out other living beings to infect, the virus is also able to somehow control the behavior of its hosts, compelling them to Follow basic instructions or act in certain ways that further the spread of the infection. This control can range from simple directives like seeking out other living beings to more complex behaviors like coordinating attacks on fortified locations" Dr Ruthven said "Shall we take a look at others?

The second individual was encased in a large cell made of an unbreakable substance. His body was covered in blood and dead skin, he didn't resemble a human at all. Parasites of various kinds were also growing in his body.

"Let me show you something," Dr Ruthven said

Dr Ruthven instructed to place a small glass cage inside his current cage. The infected easily broke the glass, and Dr Ruthven classified them as dangerous.

"How is this infection more dangerous than the previous one?" John inquired...

"You haven't seen everything yet, there are three different levels of infection,"...

John inquired. "Three levels?"....

"The infection depends on the ants as well as the host; if the infected ant has been infected for a long time, it will make the infection more dangerous for us, and if the host of the infection is strong, they will become more dangerous, resulting in level two infection," Dr Ruthven stated "Before we show you the third cage, you must be protected with some masks and specialized suits; it's a safety precaution,"

When John was about to put on the suit, a loud alarm went off.......

"What is going on here?" John asked.

"Evacuate the facility now! Everyone get out!" The doctor ordered "John, follow me now!"

John and Ruthven exited an unoccupied room, which led them to an emergency exit....

"Start the car now!" Ruthven ordered. The car had five passengers, including John and Ruthven...

"Where are we going and what is going on?" John inquired.......

"The cell broke," Ruthven replied....

"What do you mean by the cell breaking? Nothing broke, as far as I could tell" John stated....

"I never said there was only one floor full of infected people," Ruthven replied....

"What does that mean, and where is my son Mike?" John inquired......

"He was on the same floor where the alarm went off." Ruthven replied....

"What? What exactly is he doing there?" John inquired...

"We kept him in one of the cells," Ruthven said.

"You put him with the infected? Are you insane?" John inquired.......

"We didn't put him in with the infected; we put him in a small, impenetrable cell." Ruthven responded...

"If you have unbreakable cells, how did the infected escape?" John asked in a furious tone....

"I believe someone opened it," Ruthven speculated.

"This is insane, and you are all insane. What was the point of putting him there?" John inquired...

"We warned you! This was the only way to persuade you to help us," Ruthven stated....

"He's just a kid, Ruthven; he shouldn't be involved in this mess you've made!" John stated

The pain John was experiencing at the moment was the loss of his son. He had always believed in God's supremacy, believing that he would be saved in some way. "LOOK OUT!" the Driver shouted. With a loud band, the car crashed.

Mike was still trapped inside the cell. He tried looking outside, but all he saw were infected people transforming common people into one of them. Out of nowhere, an infected banged on his cell, attempting to open it, but he was unable to do so. Mike crept backwards from his cell door. "What's the matter with them?" Mike stated. He sat there, beginning to lose hope, when an infected in front of his cell fainted with a large hole in his head. Mike crept back and peered outside the cell. He saw an infected being shot in the head, and it was no longer moving....

"Get out now, come on," someone said as he unlocked the door. Mike got to his feet and followed the guy. They came to a halt by the lift after a few seconds of running, but the infected were still chasing them. "There is no time for the lift, to the stairs, come on."

Mike followed him up the stairwell. They got close to the main door, but to their surprise, it was covered with infected running around. "I know a way out; follow me." They both entered an empty room with a small exit. Mike took his time opening the door. "WATCH OUT." An infected jumped on him, but it wasn't long before the guy shot the infected. "Are you alright? Have you been bitten?".

"I'm fine. Yeah, what exactly do you mean by "bitten"? "Mike asked......

"If you are bitten by an infected, you become one of them. Come on, we have to leave right now. I will explain everything later."

When they reached at the parking area, the guy quickly grabbed his bike and told Mike to get on his bike as soon as feasible. Mike jumped in with the guy, and they both got out of the parking lot safely. The infected, on the other hand, had barred the front entrance latch. "We should take a different path. This is not going to work."

Mike pointed out a tiny gap that led to a forest; the guy observed the gap and instantly consented to go through it because they didn't have an alternative. They both took a shortcut out, passing through a broken fence that led to a forest. After some minutes, everything was going swimmingly until a loud noise came from the laboratory. They appeared to have blown up the laboratory.

Because of the large explosion, both of them fell off their bikes. The guy stood up immediately but observed Mike on the ground gripping his leg. He immediately approached him and asked if he was okay. Mike assured the guy that he had been wounded by a rock and had nothing to worry about. The guy probed the bruise and assured him that he would be OK. The man looked behind Mike and spotted a massive fire trailing them and burning down the entire forest; the fire was coming from the laboratory...

"Run! Now!"....

"But what happened?" Mike queried....

"Don't ask, just run."....

They both started running in the opposite direction of the fire and arrived near their bike. The guy picked up the bike and began driving as fast as he could. Mike took a look back and saw the entire forest burning behind them. He was scared, but he hoped he would be okay.......

"Hold on tight, we're about to go through something crazy."......

"What exactly do you mean? There is a fork in the road" Mike stated......

"There is no other way, hold on!"

They both collided with the end sign, but luckily, survived the fire.

Back at the car accident, John was alive but trapped. He slowly opened his eyes and sought to get out. He exited by smashing the door window. He wasn't badly hurt, but he did have some apparent scars....

"Are you alright?" Ruthven inquired....

"It's no surprise you're alive," John said...

"Look, John, the world is coming to an end right now. We don't have time for your joke," Ruthven responded. "What do you want me to do? You took my son, I have no idea where my daughter is, and you're telling me the world is ending" John said....

"You have a daughter?" Ruthven enquired.

"Don't you know?" John asked....

"We just found your son at your place," Ruthven explained......

"Wait a minute, what? Are you serious? "We have to find her and Mike immediately!" John stated.

"At this time?" Ruthven inquired...

"We can't abandon them, Ruthven," John said...

"We'll need to have a vehicle," Ruthven advised.

After a brief glance around, John realized he was in Mike's uncle's neighborhood. He assured Ruthven that they would grab a car. They walked to the neighborhood, and he knocked on one of the door, hoping that Mike's uncle would help because everyone was attempting to flee their homes. "Do you even have a clue who lives here?" Ruthven asked.......

"Yeah," John replied as an old lady slowly opened the door.......

John asked "Hey, is Jacob home?"

"I'm sorry, but he used to live here," the old lady replied.......

"Do you have any idea where he may be?" John inquired.......

The old lady replied, "I am sorry I can't help with that. "

"Yeah, no worries," John said "What are we going to do now?"......

They heard a lot of noise coming from behind them, so John turned around and saw a large rally of infected coming down the streets....

"We have to run Ruthven," John said as Ruthven saw the rally and advised that they should hide in the house for safety. They both knocked and requested the old lady to stay. The old woman agreed to their request and invited them both. John and Ruthven began explaining everything to her and questioned why she hadn't run away to avoid the infected, but it wasn't long before the infected began pounding on every conceivable entry into the house. John instructed the old lady to secure everything and be silent. He began preparing for the possibility that the infected would infiltrate the house. Ruthven shattered a broom and defended himself with a stick. John took the kitchen knife and other possible defense equipment.

After witnessing the infection, the old lady remained supportive, which greatly aided John and Ruthven. When the elderly lady asked how they were doing, they stated they were still fighting to keep the infected out of the house, however it was problematic considering there were hundreds of infected outsides. When the old lady watched John executing one of the infected in order to keep themselves safe and alive, she freaked out a little. The old lady tried to keep an eye out and observed a horde of infected marching towards them; she promptly informed John and Ruthven about the rally...

"You don't have enough to keep them all out." The old lady stated......

"We can't do anything else in this moment; we have no other option." John responded...

"How are we going to keep them away from us?" The old lady questioned...

"Guns, a lot of guns," Ruthven said....

"We need guns," Ruthven asked...

"You got guns?" John asked....

The old lady smiled and led them to her basement, where they discovered a slew of firearms, plenty of ammo, grenades, and everything they needed for survival......

"How the hell did you collect these things?" Ruthven questioned

"These can also come in handy; how did you obtain this?" John inquired......

"It was my husband's" the old lady stated....

The elderly lady intended to tell them about her spouse when they suddenly heard a glass crack, indicating that there may be an infected in the house....

"Ruthven, take a gun, be prepared," John said... Both John and Ruthven seized firearms and went to the corners. The elderly lady, on the other hand, unlocked a little ground door, raised a mini gun, and stood in the center.......

"Oh, good God, what do we have here? I wish you were my grandmother," Ruthven replied....

"Stay focused, Ruthven," John said.

They waited a few minutes before sensing footsteps directly from the basement stairs. John advised everyone to be prepared. "They're already on their way." There was a total fear situation for everyone, and John and Ruthven sighed as they perspired on the ground. A man with a gun stormed into the basement. He aimed his weapon at them, but after seeing three of them, he tossed his gun away and stated, "I'm not an infected person."......

"Who are you?" Ruthven asked....

"I'm Kyle, Kyle Norris"....

"What are you doing here?" John inquired.

"I noticed a horde of infected after us, so I broke in here for the safety of myself and the child," Kyle explained...

"Big mistake," the old lady said....

"It is fine, take it easy," John replied...

"Did I hear correctly that you mentioned a kid?" John asked....

"Hey kid, come down here," Kyle yelled.

The kid came down gradually, he was terrified, and as he moved down, he recognized John and was pleasantly surprised. It was Mike. He raced to John with happiness, and John did the same. It appeared that John had found his kid, but Sally was still missing...

"Mike, you're still alive. How did you get away?" John said as Mike pointed at Kyle before saying, "Kyle helped me."....

"Thank you," John said relieved after making slow eye contact with Kyle.

Mike casted a brief glance at Ruthven and was scared and perplexed to see him with John; afterwards, John cast a peek at Ruthven but told Mike not to talk to him and to concentrate on escaping. Kyle grinned for a few seconds until they heard a loud band outside their door. Kyle hurriedly advised them to go since he spotted another large horde approaching their way, and the infected would be much stronger than the last horde.

"I hope everyone has stocked up." Before turning to stare at Kyle, John stated, "You better load up and don't betray us."

Kyle smiled softly before nodding his head. He began loading; while loading, he saw an undisturbed large black box on the corner; he opened the box and discovered a brief note and a grenade; he seized both and hurried upstairs. Kyle discovered John and Ruthven battling to keep the infected at bay, he rushed to the front entrance and supported them in blocking it. The infected kept banging on the door unconsciously. John and Ruthven took a deep breath before ordering everyone to use another exit as soon as possible. Kyle approached John and informed him that the back yard from where he and Mike had broken in was completely vacant. John dashed to the backyard, knowing there was no other way to escape the infected while keeping Mike safe. They all hurried to the back yard, only to discover that the infected had followed Kyle and Mike and had now completely engulfed the backyard.

They stared at the infected as the infected rushed towards them; after a short time, the infected had successfully entered the property and began to act erratically. For the first time in his life, John was terrified of death, and he glanced at Mike, knowing he had little to no chance of survival.

They were trapped in a position where anybody could easily discover them, but the unconscious infected found it tough. The old lady appeared to be relentless. "How are we going to get out of here?" Ruthven inquired......

"She knows something," John said, looking at the old lady, while pointing his finger at her. The old lady saw them and immediately started running, and everyone else followed her, causing the infected to run like maniacs. "Where are we going?" John screamed

More and more infected broke into the house, the whole place became infested in minutes. Ruthven was at the last attempting to cling on, he started firing at the infected to buy time for himself and others but unexpectedly paused, he made eye contact with one of the infected, it seemed like he recognized that individual and couldn't shoot, John quickly grabbed that infected and threw him down as he began blocking the path with shattered objects. They had finally arrived to the backyard; John was weary, as were the others; Mike held John's hand. John began to have optimism for their survival, but there was one thing that bothered him: Sally's survival. Because the infected were not stopping, John took a close look at Kyle from head to toe and instructed him to take Mike with him and escape. Kyle stayed mute and glanced at Mike, imploring him to come.

Mike, on the other hand, did not like the notion and hurried to John, declaring, "We will not abandon you!"

"You must leave; we have no other choice." With a sorrowful but confident expression, John told Mike.

Kyle went gently and grabbed Mike's hand, telling him to come, Mike said his goodbyes, and they ran off via the backyard. John pursued them across the backyard, attempting to hold off the infected with the protection of the old lady and Ruthven....

"When I say go, you get through the valley," John ordered as Kyle began to move carefully....

"We can't abandon them." Mike stated quietly...

"Who said we were going to abandon them?" Kyle responded quietly as Mike gave a little smile and they both began moving forward. With a loud bang, the infected began swarming the area. John ordered Kyle to take Mike and run, but Kyle grabbed Mike and flung him to the other side safely, then ran towards the infected to defend everyone. "KYLE". Shouted John

He raced towards him to save him from the horde of infected, but just as he was about to reach him, Kyle removed the grenade from his pocket, withdrew the safety ring, and tossed it. John stepped back and told everyone to leap from the fence. Fortunately, all of them survived. John obtained a broad view of the flaming home, which had been set ablaze by a grenade and was engulfing all of the infected within.

When a guy leaped from a fence, Mike got a closer look and saw that it was Kyle, who was covered with infected and was constantly burning. John helped him and they were all relieved to see him, but the rally of infected wasn't finished yet; all the infected began racing over and jumping to get them. They all had enough time to get away from them, so they strolled away like movie stars while the entire home was on fire.

Kyle proposed going into one of the cars and grabbing it as they came to a halt on a roadway full of damaged vehicles and infected everywhere. John agreed, and they proceeded to the nearest car. It was a little blue car that could fit all of them...

"Mike, you remain here with her and let us in." John proposed it since there were too many infected and it may be risky for Mike....

"OK, yeah," Mike replied"

"Don't be afraid, Mike. Keep your head up, "John stated.

He looked him in the eyes. "Now, once I pass by here, you immediately jump in my car. It won't be long until the infected arrive. There's no time to waste." John gave the directive. Kyle moved to the left, Ruthven to the right, and John to the back. There was an infected on the front. John advised killing it with something silent to avoid attracting more infected.

John stabbed him to death with his knife. They followed the same pattern of coming behind infected and executing them. John took the car and told Kyle to sit in the front with a firearm. Ruthven sat in the rear, opening the door for Mike and the old lady. Because they lacked keys, John attempted to start the car. John began by wielding a knife and a little pointed rod... "Is this even plausible?" Kyle stated softly.

John nodded his head, delivering his answer to Kyle, and tried to start the automobile again, he seemed so determined to start the car....

"Sorry to bother you, but I believe we have a problem." Ruthven stated....

"What really is it?" Kyle said

It only took Kyle a few seconds to peek out the rear window and observe a massive swarm of infected racing towards them. "We must go ASAP! JOHN!"

Kyle yelled as he spotted the infected getting closer and closer, gathering other infected along the way. When John heard Kyle screaming, he hurried to start the car. The infected were coming closer and closer, Mike and the old lady were watching the horde racing down the road to the car, she swiftly drew out her firearm and shot at a random car, causing the car alarm to beep, giving John some time to continue his task. After several efforts, the car started with a loud thud, and John, Ruthven, and Kyle were overjoyed.

They swiftly rode the car near the old lady and Mike and drove away, while the infected hounded them like madmen. They drew away, but two of the infected clung to the rear of the car, attracting more of them. This attracted John's attention, and seeing it made him even more concerned. The old lady urged that she look after them. She then told them to open the rear door, after which she shot both infected in the head, killing them...

"Wow that was quick. Nice work." Kyle said...
"Where are we going, John?" Ruthven inquired...
"We're heading to my place," John informed...
"What is the point of getting there? Every family is fleeing this awful city, and if we stay any longer, our lives may be jeopardized; you saw how barely we escaped" Ruthven proposed...

"You may go now if you don't want to come," John stated as he stopped the car and turned back to Ruthven...

"I'm taking my daughter with me; anyone have any problems?" John asked.

The Undead Bonds

John drove up to his house and walked right in. He proposed Kyle take charge of the wheels and wait for him to return. When John entered, he saw that every single door was open, and it smelt terrible. John was drawn to Sally's room by the smell. It smelled like a dead guy, and John hoped it wasn't Sally.

He entered and discovered an infected guy in her bed with a large iron rod on his head....

"Sally, Sally! Where are you? "John shouted.

John spotted blood drips on the floor and tracked them to the back yard. It appeared that she had fled the house on her own or that she had been abducted. John alerted Mike, and they both searched the whole house but were unable to trace anything. Mike discovered a tiny message from Sally in which she suggested fleeing. It was close to the television. The television was still on and was showing a report on the infected growing. They thought she fled away on her own, which increased John's concern for her...

"Are you okay, Dad?" Mike inquired...

"Just give me a little time," John explained...

"We have to go, dad, there's a horde following us all the way through," Mike urged....

"What's the matter, John? Come on, we need to get moving or we'll all perish." Kyle said

The old lady jumped out of her car and began shooting the infected who were coming at them. Kyle was agitated, so he grabbed John and began dragging him towards the car, but it was too late. The infected had already gathered around him. The old lady was doing well until a large infected leapt on her from above, which caused Kyle to drop John and run towards her, killing the infected swiftly, but he was too late,

The infected had bit the old lady, she noticed her mark and then looked at Kyle. "Oh, what's going on?" Ruthven inquired...

"How serious is it?" John inquired...

"What are you talking about?" Ruthven questioned. "This," John replied, pointing his finger to the old lady's bite; when Ruthven saw this, he stepped out of his car and stood in dread...

"How were you bitten?" Ruthven inquired...

"It's not important; just tell us if she'll live and what we should do next." John inquired…

"It's an infected bite; there's nothing we can do, John." Ruthven stated as Kyle interrupted and said, "What are we supposed to do now? We don't have a lot of time." "I'm so sorry, but we have to leave her." Ruthven stated "What the hell are you saying? We can't leave her in this condition with all these infected people". John was enraged.

"Listen to me, John, I don't want to leave her either, but look around you, all of this has been done by infected, they are killing all the humans and she is going to be one of them and we can't change it, she is going to become an infected sooner or later and our lives are already in danger, and I don't want to be feared anymore." Ruthven stated

John stood in silence.

"He's correct, I was already a burden; I mean, I'm old, and I wouldn't have been able to help you much in the future." The elderly lady stated while everyone had a sad expression on their faces, Kyle's eyes were a little wet, and they stood there in silence. They all heard a huge bang and were promptly aroused; they searched around but found nothing strange.

Ruthven indicated that there are infected people around and that they should leave this city as soon as possible. They all bid their goodbyes to the old lady and rushed into the car.

They all drove away in a car, and the old lady entered the house, attempting to save herself and their life by covering them. One of the hazardous infected that entered the house afterwards disturbed her. She did everything to protect herself but failed. She believed she was dead, but then she had an idea. She noticed a fan just over the infected and shot it. That gave her enough time to flee. When she opened the rear door, she saw a long, deserted road. She began sprinting in one of them, but then she spotted something. She saw her spouse as one of the infected, stooped for a second, and then bolted; it was one of her darkest fears. She couldn't get the feeling that her spouse was one of those aiming to murder her after a few steps. As she ran, she was overtaken by infected people, including her husband. She couldn't handle it any longer and chose to commit herself since she refused to become one of them.

"If today is my final day, I know I won't die because of you morons." the elderly lady stated

It was a tragic conclusion for her, but John and his entourage fled the city. They left town and stopped at a local gas station to relax for a few moments before continuing on their journey.

FOUR

7 Years Later

After seven years, they were living in a military quarantine zone. They had to complete the things that were required of them if they wished to dwell in that location. Mike needed to learn about the infected and how they could protect themselves. It appeared to be enjoyable, but the training carried a considerable danger of harm. John, on the other hand, had to ensure that the gates were always kept safe from the infected. Ruthven and Kyle were tasked with removing all infected from their assigned region. Everyone has some sort of task to complete. There was no time to relax. They don't get together for dinner till seven, this carried on for a long period of time. The new day had barely begun, and Ruthven and Kyle were on the search for the infected when they noticed a mother and a teenage girl being chased by an infected.

Kyle shot him in the head, but he was also taken aback by how they managed to escape the quarantined zone. The mother thanked Kyle and Ruthven and ran into the quarantine zone. They tried to reach her but were ambushed by infected. Kyle instantly shot them and turned around, but the mother and her daughter had fled inside the quarantine zone....

"We should keep a look out for her, but first let's get going since we have infected to kill." Ruthven stated

They began moving on their feet; the path was pretty long, so Ruthven started talking to Kyle to lighten the mood. Ruthven was still with John and everyone else. Since time has changed drastically and the behaviour has also changed in Ruthven, these seven years have taught a lot of stuff to everyone. Mike was 15 and was still learning. All the survivors, when they turn 18, get some kind of task to help the camp, but until then they have to attend what they call their military school.

"How was your night?" Ruthven enquired...

"Pretty rough, couldn't sleep," Kyle replied.

Apparently, a huge storm passed through the night, disrupting everyone's sleep and turning the night into an infected-attacked chaos; most of the military guarded tents were destroyed by the storm, and the rest were attacked by the remaining infected; the military attempted to take control of the infected, but many of them died while protecting the survivors; it was the night that will be remembered by all.

As Ruthven and Kyle continued on their customary path, they came across an abandoned home. As they would on any other day, they walked inside and cleared the infected within....

"I suppose that's all for today." Ruthven stated...

"We should head back now". Ruthven said

Kyle was staring off into the distance when Ruthven saw he wasn't paying attention. He swiftly approached him and placed his hands on his shoulder, saying,

"What's going on?"....

"We must flee." Kyle said....

"Is it because of that mother that you want to go back so quickly?" Ruthven inquired....

"NO, we have been ambushed; we must return now and alert others." Kyle stated this and instantly began running. Ruthven had no idea what Kyle was talking about at first; apparently, Kyle suspected that they were all about to be ambushed, so he instructed Ruthven to rush and notify everyone. Both of them began running, and they weren't far from the military zone when they were greeted by the infected on their way back. Kyle took off quickly, leaving a large gap between him and Ruthven; he kept clearing all the infected along the way making things easier for Ruthven, who was eventually able to catch up with Kyle. They arrived at the military quarantine zone and were welcomed by John, who was deployed at the front main gate. Kyle dashed through without waiting for John and yelled, "WE HAVE BEEN AMBUSHED!"

The smile suddenly faded from John's face while the military gave instructions to form a squad and assemble at the front entrance, instructing youngsters to remain in the tent for their own protection. They formed a crew although they needed one more person with them, they looked around while everyone gathered at the front gate, Kyle spotted the mother who he saved earlier, he called her and they all ran towards the front gate with lots of guns and ammunitions. There was utter stillness for a few seconds, everyone was still standing in the same posture, all the military guards were looking about, attempting to locate anyone they could, but all the places were clear, and they didn't discover anything or anybody. The military told the survivors to go to their tents, but they were all still searching..."All of you go to your tents, in case of emergency we will call you, so be ready." The military ordered

The survivors were still standing still, nobody budged, John and his squad were also in the same position, instantaneously two of the survivors started moving towards their tent, when they both looked back everyone blankly stared at them, in next few seconds two bullets were fired killing both of the survivors, this began a big conflict among the survivors and the shots began to fire within the few seconds, every survivor started getting attacked, Special forces guards were unable to locate the survivors. During the ambush, the front gate was completely destroyed, allowing a large number of infected to enter the quarantine zone.

The remaining survivors panicked as they saw the infected around them, and the military kept failing and failing to locate the ambushers while also saving the people, they kept dying. At this point, John and his squad were still alive after taking cover behind the ridge. He searched for ways to retreat, but each time he attempted to get out of cover, ambushers were always waiting to fire near them, pressuring John's squad to remain where they are....

"Now what are we supposed to do?" Ruthven stated. "I have a solution." Kyle said as he peered into the eyes of John and Ruthven. John was perplexed, but Ruthven seemed to understand the strategy Kyle wished to carry out. "Where is she?" Ruthven inquired while Kyle looked around but she was nowhere to be found, and John seemed to have entirely missed what Kyle was talking about......

"John! What happened to the lady that joined our squad?" Kyle inquired......

"I don't know Kyle, and is it really that big of a deal?" John said......

"John, she might be able to get us out." Kyle said "What?" John asked, puzzled....

"She was able to sneak out of this quarantine zone without any guard noticing, and today not only did we watch her get out, but she also returned inside without being spotted by the military personnel." Kyle elaborated.......

"It's impossible, but even if we have a small possibility of escaping, I'm willing to do it." John stated......

"Hey! Kyle! I believe I see her!" Ruthven stated.

"What is she doing there?" Kyle said "I'm heading there, and you guys cover me."

Kyle rapidly followed the mother and spotted her with her daughter; he asked her why she had left them behind and come here all alone in danger....

"We don't have time to explain it; do you want to come out with us? Think immediately". Mother stated.

"HEY! JOHN! We are running out of time, so hurry up." Kyle yelled.

John tried to take a peek back for the ambushers, but every time he tried to peak, the ambushers attacked him, making it hard for John to escape his current situation. John did his hardest to flee as fast as possible but failed every time; the ambushers continued to strike and even made him bleed once due to a little wound on John's hand. When Kyle noticed John was trapped and struggling, he hurriedly requested the mother to wait for just a couple of minutes since John needed his help; nonetheless, the mother waited for Kyle to return. Kyle raced towards John, which astonished him; he instantly turned and asked Kyle that what he was doing here and urged him to escape immediately....

"What? I'm not abandoning you, John ". Kyle said. "Why did you come here? We're both completely stuck now ". John stated "How are we supposed to get away from them?"

Kyle began to look around for a while and observed that all of the survivors residing in the quarantine zone were dead and lying on the ground, so he immediately tried lifting the corpse and slowly putting him on his back, he then took the angle and cover of the ridge and managed to run, the ambushers observed this and instantly fired shots, but all of the bullets were struck by the corpse, leaving Kyle unharmed and safe. Kyle advised John to do the same, so John immediately followed Kyle and ran with him, successfully fleeing their position. When they got close to the mother and her daughter's tent, they found out that no one was there...

"Where is everyone, and where is Ruthven?" John inquired......

"They can't abandon us like this!" Kyle said...

"They already have," John stated...

"No, no, no, I don't believe it," Kyle stated...

"Look around you Kyle and tell me what you're seeing. In each and every step there are survivors begging for their lives, begging to live, begging God to end this, everything is unfolding, this world didn't end because of the collapse of civilization, it ended when humans lost faith in humanity, when humans stopped trusting others, when they stopped forgiving, when they began fighting for their preservation and their odds of enduring in this apocalyptic world." John said as Kyle and John were ready to give up when they heard a voice say, "DAD." Mike was standing there as John turned around. They witnessed Ruthven following him. It appeared like they had regained hope of survival.

John grabbed Mike tight and asked him if he was doing okay. Both were delighted to see each other and were very happy...

"I'm sorry to interrupt your father-son bonding, but we're now under siege and if we don't leave immediately, we'd be better off dead," Kyle said.

"All right, follow me, I'll show you the way," Ruthven stated

Kyle and John were stunned and startled to learn that Ruthven knew a path out of the invaded quarantine zone. Ruthven snatched the gun that had belonged to the military guards slain in the shooting and counselled John and Kyle to do the likewise for their own protection. They all stuck together and abided by Ruthven's route, wordlessly they were able to traverse all the sight-seeing and proceeded their way towards the large containers that were presumed to be packed with food and survival gear for the entire domicile in case of emergencies, however, it was vacant and they all managed to learn that the military might have told lies to them and that there was no food for one's preservation in the coming years. While still on their path, Ruthven persuaded them to travel through a narrow opening inside the insulated container, which brought them to an unknown wooded region devoid of infected, where they were pleasantly surprised to find the mother and her daughter awaiting them. Kyle questioned her, without hesitancy, "Why were you intending to leave the quarantine zone?"

She remained silent for several seconds before asserting that she had been working inside the food zone and that she encountered the food crisis a long time ago, and she even attempted to explain to the military guards about the shortfall, which provoked the guard, toward which they initially responded, "We don't have any other sources, keep on working today and we would command you yet further."

The Undead Bonds

Kyle was outraged by the military's response, but he wasn't shocked; at this juncture, Ruthven, John, and Mike were all listening to what she was saying. She continued her statement by mentioning something that startled every person in the place: "The military directed me to continue preparing whatever was left, and once the entire food item is gone, report the authorities straight away. They were going to substitute the animal flesh with human meat, which would constitute everyone as cannibalistic."

After knowing what the military intended to carry out in the near term, they discovered reasons why she was attempting to flee the quarantine zone. They all agreed, however, the dilemma was that they didn't even know where to head and seemed to have no strategy. John persisted the conversation by asking, "Where we all are intended to go? The entire area is brutally attacked."

The mother slowly managed to open her daughter's shoulder bag, started opening the pocket, and making a cantankerous sound she lifted out a custom-crafted map with several red marked circles. The mother pointed her finger at the map's top and then said, "We are as of now outside of this quarantine zone, which also means that we need to travel all the way there."

She trailed her finger from top to bottom, referring to a location labelled "UnMarked." The location was labelled with a red circle, accompanied by various yellow and blue arrows; the location was not that far away, although it was not a reasonable distance that could easily be accomplished by foot. John inquired about the UnMarked with the mother.

"This was an old facility that was utilized to discover the remedy for the infectious disease; however, it wasn't long before it was run over by the infected, and also to our poor luck, the security and defensive systems failed to make a change. A while back my husband was capable of capturing this vast territory which can presumably hold more survivors than this quarantine zone," she replied "You will always get food, ammunition, and emergency aid, in addition to an enhancement in our and your likelihood of survival."

This interaction intrigued John and others, so they told her that they would be eager to help her with her journey in exchange for food as well as other perks. She vehemently acknowledged and briefed them about the approach she had devised a long time prior.

Since the journey was expected to be so lengthy, the mother advised them that the primary and most crucial task was to assist her in finding a vehicle, and the rest would be simple.

"HANDS IN THE AIR".

The hollering came from behind the containers, it appeared that the entire quarantine zone had been ransacked by the flanking maneuvers and one of them had snuck back his way over here, he instantly aimed his firearm at them, and they all glanced at each other thinking that since he was the sole they would indeed be capable of capturing out such a single individual and yet everyone knew deep down that even if they attempted to shoot him, somebody from theirs might end up dead or severely injured.

John was willing to lay down his life, however, there was one issue that held him back: throwing other people's lives in jeopardy.

The Undead Bonds

He pondered this for a long time until he devised a means to divert his attention away from the mother and her daughter. He began talking to the ambusher who had crept in, and he was successful in diverting his attention away from the Mother and her daughter. The ambusher slowly approached John, pointing directly at his head, and came increasingly closer till he reached a moment within which he positioned his weapon at John's head.

During this spot, anybody could have killed the ambusher, but they felt sure that if they interrupted, John will indeed end up dying. Nobody was willing to take this shot, so they all stood there meekly, and the ambusher appeared dead in John's sight. They initiated direct eye contact, which elicited a wide range of feelings in everybody's presence. The mother had a clear opportunity to strike the ambusher; she recognized the worst-case scenario, but she promptly drew her firearm and aimed squarely at the ambusher's head... "Drop your weapon RIGHT NOW! I will give you five seconds," Mother stated unequivocally.

The ambusher remained still, did not flinch, and did not utter a single word; Ruthven and Kyle gazed at the ambusher, suppressing the need to attack him; the mother demanded anew, "DROP NOW," and she began counting; 5 "
She continued to count. "4"....
This lacked an effect on the ambusher; he maintained eye contact, and Mother kept counting, "3."...
 "2" and the last time "1" ... The trigger was pulled and a shot was fired. The place fell silent, and the mother was the most surprised, as she was not the person who fired the shot. John's head was splattered with blood, while the ambusher's weapon tumbled to the ground shortly after the shot was fired.

The intruder was slain. Everyone was stunned when the ambusher's head was blown out by one of his kind.

They all looked back at the entrance through which they had come, and a man was standing there with his rifle. "Get out of here before more people arrive. The entire place has been obliterated," he said. "Go immediately, or you will all die."

Being one of the most confident people, John recognized that this was not the battle to engage in because they had a mother and her sole child who, even if they could, were incapable of taking on an entire group. "We should flee because who knows how many people are in there." According to John

When they all began to move, John stepped forward to make room and then accompanied the mother to follow her directions. When Ruthven turned back and noticed the ambusher, who had flashed him a little grin and was now walking away, he didn't quite understand that but proceeded to move forward anyways. As they passed through the tall woods, they all heard someone yelling and instantly concluded that they had been deceived by the ambushers and were being pursued. John spotted an enormous rod hiding something, he swiftly commanded everyone to hid themselves behind the large rod, waiting for the right opportunity to react. They were accompanied by the mother and her daughter. The ambushers commenced to encircle them, passing each one after the other. John observed something disguised by the foliage and little shafts. He immediately commanded everyone to move out of that zone whilst discarding all the leaves concealing that opening.

Upon clearing in there, he leaped alone to ensure that they were able to continue their expedition from there.

The hole led to the basement of an ancient room. John unlocked the door, but he was accosted by an infected who was waiting for him on the opposite side. This garnered Kyle's attention, and he instantly stepped in and freed John. They all followed Kyle into the basement and discovered a horrid thing, a heap of infected covering that appeared to be the sole exit. "Leave this to me," Kyle said as he leaped in, racking up a few decent strikes before calling for help. Ruthven accompanied him and cleared all the infected. They were trying to avoid making any commotion because the ambushers could find them and strike at any time..."That was a good strike Ruthven," Kyle commended before dragging the infected aside. The mother was horrified, but her daughter appeared to lack expression upon witnessing the slaughtering of the infected, which aroused a slight thought in John's head, but he eventually stepped further toward Kyle and Ruthven to plan their next action.

"I suppose there's someone at the top," Kyle said as he began to interact. "Do you reckon that they located us, the ambushers?" Ruthven Joined. The movement they all felt was unnerving, and their hearts began to race. They were all hoping that the ambushers would abandon them and allow them to continue their journey, but they weren't afraid to carry the battle with them; it appeared that they were ready for almost anything.

"I suppose it's too late; they've already arrived," Kyle stated that and John had already put a strong strategy in place as he was the one studying the area and was primed and ready for the invasion. He collected everyone and explained the plan as quickly as he possibly could, and by happenstance, everyone understood what he was referring to.

They swiftly positioned themselves and awaited for the action to begin. Sluggishly, one of the ambushers leaped through, the entire place was spherical, so one human could barely see a significant chunk of it at a moment, when he jumped, he discovered that the entire place looked vacant, behind him was John lurking, he decided to wait for the moment when the ambusher moved out of sight as he was standing just beneath the opening. The ambusher went towards the front with a squeak, and so did John from behind. The entire area appeared to be deserted, with no disturbances to be observed. John kept a good range at the outset to acquire a strong position and a stronger grip. Everyone else was hiding at this stage. John discreetly seized and beheaded the ambusher. The other ambushers were still awake. They tried reaching the ambusher who had jumped in, but there was no answer. After a few more attempts, they were quite concerned and decided to dive in alone. They prepared one of the ambushers and assisted him in getting inside, just as they assisted the other ambushers. The very moment the ambusher walked in, he was caught by John and quickly decapitated.

The ambusher witnessed him falling over but did not respond when he shouted his name. They tried calling him twice, however, this time there was no reply. They all formed a crew to enter and examine what was going off, but before that, they chose to hurl a grenade inside to ensure that no entity remains. They hastily retreated for cover, moments after dropping the grenade. Just when they anticipated and had scheduled the grenade to explode, there was neither sound nor evidence of exploding. This perplexed the ambushers, who were still lurking and expected the bomb to explode shortly.

When the ambushers saw there was no explosion, they dashed toward the opening, and everyone swiftly prepared to go in full force. They all rushed in and rapidly endeavored to cover the entire area, but all they witnessed was a huge space until they spotted someone heading towards them, it was John. He approached them slowly and unafraid. The ambushers slowly turned and stood across from John, their rifles loaded and pointing squarely at him, "Why are you all here? There's no place for people like you," John remarked solemnly, adding, "I ask you to turn and walk away for your good.".... "You can't kill us, we have more people, we are quicker, we are larger, and we have advanced firepower," the ambusher said, keeping eye contact with John....... "And you still lose," John added. He was instantly interrupted by the ambusher's loud chuckle.

He pointed confidently at John and instructed him to leave his sight because he is going to offer him a chance to flee only for exhibiting excellent confidence. The ambusher's presumed John was withdrawing until they observed he was moving in the opposite direction. They promptly screamed out to John, but he did not react and continued walking. Ambushers were confused but still held their positions as John approached the end and gradually bent down near a rock-filled area and drew out a long rifle. This end, John was reloading his weapon, and as soon as he finished, he targeted the nearest ambusher and executed him without squandering a second. This shot resulted in ambushers and John blasting away at one another. He quickly hid around the same rock fill area in which he had tucked away his rifle, and just as the ambushers assumed they had captured John, there was a big explosion, which disclosed the entire John's crew attacking from across all vantage points, covering the entire group of ambushers.

"DROP YOUR WEAPONS NOW," Kyle yelled, and John added, "You heard him drop your weapons, you're surrounded from every position." John finished slowly. Hard eye contact was held at that moment among John and the entire crew of the ambushers. John stared at them gallantly and started walking towards them with a rifle by his side. Throughout this moment, the ambushers knew they had no choice but to drop weapons as they were trapped in the middle and surrounded by John and his crew.

When John passed by the ambushers, they lowered their weapons, and every member of the ambushers crew was looking at a single person, John was approaching briskly, and Kyle and Ruthven started closing in from behind. John sensed the ambushers' fury and kept moving till he was close to him. The two exchanged stares until John seized the weapon from the ambusher's grasp and flung it

It's the end," John declared, "and now I'm the one offering you a chance to run away. Don't waste time because if it runs out, you die, my friend. "You heard him, leave! There is still time." Kyle muttered from behind......

"It's not over my friend, the day will come when I'll make you beg for it, and you will remember me by the name Muhammad." and he fled.

Kyle sighed and gazed at Ruthven as they both began loading the weapons that the ambushers had left over. John, on the other hand, began investigating the ambusher's corpse, discovering some first aid and water that was insufficient even for one person. John grabbed the bottle and tried to get everyone's attention by saying loudly, "We don't have enough supplies, and therefore we're considering keeping an eye out for supplies on our journey."

The Undead Bonds

Everyone glanced at each other and agreed unquestioningly. Kyle interrupted and revealed an abandoned highway that goes the same way as they were meant to take, which they uncovered while going for reconnaissance. "We should find enough supplies to live on this day," he added....

John brought up a map and located the route and connecting bridges described by Kyle. When he said yes, he established odd eye contact. They walked through the forest for a few minutes before arriving at one of the highways that appeared to be abandoned. Nobody had visited here in years. "Find some supplies and get moving; the survivor didn't have enough," John said.......

When John spotted a few vehicles close, he decided to call Mike for help. He called and told him to clear out some cars, to which Mike agreed and carried on. John was preparing to search for something when he recognized someone with Mike. He found the mother's daughter and approached her, asking her, "What is your name?" She answered, "Anna."

".Hey, John, I've got something for you; look. See, there's a radio," Kyle added. "Do you believe anyone is still there?" When Ruthven arrived and asked, John noticed the radio and attempted to hear and absorb any information he could. "What exactly is going on? Boys?" Ruthven inquired, to which John answered, "We located a functional radio."

"Do you believe it will be important?" Ruthven asked, his gaze drawn to John, who was struggling to mend the radio......

"What exactly do you mean? Are there any survivors who can link with us?" John inquired, and Ruthven responded. "I mean, Jhonnyyy, you should be the one answering that."

"If you think this is simple, come try it yourself, and don't call me that again," John retorted fiercely.

Slow footfall was heard, and a group was approaching. None realized it since they were so focused on mending the radio. Slowly, they reached a position where the survivors could quickly take them over; they swiftly concealed behind a car, and one of the members, clad entirely in blue and holding a long gun, appeared to be the leader of their group; he instructed one of them to take hostage, anyone, he could have. One of the members spotted Mike struggling to unlock the vehicle and gradually crept up to him, and as Mike was about to approach Anna for a backup, which was in the contrary direction, the survivor snatched him and fired a round into the air to grab every one's attention....

"NO, NO, NO!" John dashed to Mike but was abruptly halted when he noticed the guy holding Mike had placed a knife around his neck and warned, "One more step and your little kid dies."

John's eyes were turning red since his only thought was to see Mike safely, which was difficult for anybody to comprehend. John hollered at him, asking what he was looking for......

"Some food, I guess; we've been starving, so let's make this clear, you give us the food and other supplies, and we leave this little boy right here, or we come down and slaughter this young kid of yours, and we destroy all of you," he continued, "How does this sound."

The guy asked him again; however, just as he was saying something, he was cut short by none other than Anna. She took her revolver from her bag and pointed it precisely at his head; thankfully, she had gotten behind him briefly. The guy saw it as a joke and began laughing like a madman.

He cracked a few jokes about her, which made Anna irate. This enjoyable chat didn't continue long, and he was shot by Anna who swiftly saved Mike and went behind the car for refuge.

This resulted in a massive shootout between John and the dead guy's crew. Mercifully, Mike was safe, which gave John a sigh of relief, but the danger was still upon them. The dead guy's crew was wandering around them and spraying bullets, so John took a risk and blasted out one of the cars by accident as there was still some fuel left, which caused an enormous outburst which killed a large number of people but also attracted a large number of infected with it. They all eliminated the remaining survivors and sat down to catch their breath when they were startled by radio static, "Hello, hello, unit 7, hey" static on the radio....

"Somebody seems to be contacting these dead survivors. Come on in, folks," Kyle said...

"What did you do already?" Ruthven murmured, gazing at John.......

"Don't think too quickly," Kyle stated. "It looks like their team is contacting them,"

"We better hurry; they could be looking for them," John suggested......

"He's correct; we should relocate," Ruthven agreed. "Some of these cars still have gas in them, I think some vehicles aren't that old," John replied as Anna and Mike approached him. Once John saw him, he first asked whether he was well, and then he complimented Anna for helping him and, in specific ways, protecting everybody. When Kyle yelled, "The infected are coming!" the conversation abruptly came to an end. "Oh crap, we need to hurry." While rushing towards the vehicles where they anticipated they might find some gas and it might work,

John stated that they weren't sure but still held hope. They located a functional car on their first attempt. They quickly gathered all of their firearms and supplies and climbed in. The car was tiny, so they had to adapt. The swarm of infected successfully pursued them just as they started their vehicle, and all of them immediately took over the car and began bashing the windshield. Kyle was already aware of the sunroof, so he started by opening it and spraying the infected with bullets. Fortunately, he was able to destroy a portion of the infected that were required to die to move the vehicle. John started the car swiftly and drove straight without stopping. They soon caught up to the highway and continued on their route. John pulled out the map and marked all the probable trails he thought were feasible.

This abruptly stopped when John encountered an unexpected traffic barrier on the deserted highway. He promptly came to a halt, causing Ruthven to collide with the front of the vehicle....

"Why did you stop, ahh, my nose?" Ruthven inquired.
"John, what happened?" Kyle questioned...
"There's a roadblock," John said....
"Has it been blocked on purpose?" Ruthven inquired. "I can't say,"

As John approached the blockage, a gunshot was fired near his leg as a warning. He turned back and saw a bunch of survivors aiming at them; he realized it would be a difficult battle to win, so he started speaking to them. "Hey! Man, we want to cross the street. What's the big deal?" John asked...

"Not so quick; you must pay up." a survivor stated.
"What exactly do you mean?" John inquired......

"Fifty bullets, pay up or leave." a survivor stated as Kyle and Ruthven stepped out of the vehicle and told the mother and her daughter Anna to stay in the car and be with Mike. John smirked and glanced back at his crew. They all gazed at each other blankly until Ruthven suggested, "There's no point fighting them; we have people to protect, Mike, Anna, and her Mother. They can't battle an entire crew like this." He muttered. "Fine, get the bullets," John said, nodding.

Ruthven dashed to their car as John and Kyle stood still, staring at the survivors above them who were barring the highway. Ruthven returned with a box full of ammunition and tossed it to John. He took the box and began heading towards them, instructing Kyle and Ruthven to return to their car and keep it running. He passed the box over to the survivor. Anna was not a stable girl; she kept questioning Kyle about whatever was going on at every turn, to which Kyle answered, "Nothing is going on, so put your seatbelts on and get ready."......

"There you go, now let us pass."...

"Of course, would you mind if I ask you something?" "What happened now?"....

"We want to borrow your ride."...

"Nah that's not possible?" John responded...

"Look around you, we outnumber you Mr cool guy, you don't possibly have a choice."....

"We can't possibly offer you our ride. We just gave you what you asked for," John said....

"I'm sorry, but this isn't how it's supposed to work. Go, you have five minutes before everyone dies," said the survivor.

He returned to explain everything. Anna suggested shooting them, but he explained that it was impossible and that they should simply hand it to them since they had no other alternative.

Nobody wanted to say yes, but they realized they had no choice. "There you have it." While tossing the car keys to the survivor above, John remarked. Half of the survivors took the vehicle, while the other half stayed behind in their second car. When John and all others noticed the vehicle driving down the road, Ruthven became irritated and said, "GODDAMIT, What the hell?" Anna began to grin broadly; the cause of this smile was not Ruthven but something else; John sensed something and glanced at Anna, comprehending something. "Everyone get ready to shoot," John yelled immediately......

"What happened, John?"

While the survivors were driving, the car exploded with a tremendous explosion. With only half of the survivors remaining, John commanded, "Kill them all." When John looked at the survivor, he smiled, signalling they had won.......

"How did that thing blow up?" Ruthven asked, somewhat perplexed, looking at Anna. John burst out laughing. This irritated Ruthven even more, prompting him to yell, "What's so funny about it?" Kyle laughed as well, and Anna ultimately admitted that she had placed a grenade in that thing shortly before they departed. Ruthven seemed puzzled and inquired, "Then why didn't it explode sooner?"...

"I had something linked to it, like a rope." Anna reacted with a smile. When John observed Mike's somber expression, he instantly altered his mood and instructed everyone to get supplies. He added, "Let's inspect this surviving car. It appears enormous."...

"I'm not going to lie. That's a nice car," Ruthven said...

"All right, let's see whether this has enough gas," John remarked...

"Argh,"......

"What's going on now, John?" Ruthven said. "We're out of gas, even less than on our last ride," Kyle explained. "Do you know where we can get fuel?".

"I'm not sure," John answered, "but I suppose he knew where to find gas."....

"Who? The dead survivor?" Kyle inquired...

"Yeah," John said, "I kind of questioned him about the gas when handing over the box of bullets. "..

"You knew he'd laugh at you rather than provide you the place to get fuel," Kyle said...

"Yes, he warned me you're not going to get it with such confidence," John responded....

"He said you couldn't get gas, and you assume he knew, but wait, I'm confused," Kyle added....

"Yes, he could have known and intended to collect all the gas himself. They needed that car because they did not have enough gas. "For gas," John said, "and also because only half of them had left, for gas right."

"Wow, that's a lot of Gas." Kyle asked, "What are we doing now?"....

"We're tracking where that car was heading," John explained......

."Man, it better be worth it," Ruthven remarked. So, they started the car and continued on their journey. They accelerated and peeked out the window....

"It was the most horrible death someone could experience," Ruthven added....

"Well, they got what they deserved," Anna remarked. "Hah, I like this gal," Ruthven commented.

John grinned slightly and continued on his way, noticing that the road was not visible and that something was up the road. He immediately informed everyone that there was something up ahead. They all peered out the window and saw they were a large group of infected. John swiftly instructed Kyle to determine the size of the horde...

"Yeah yeah, hold for a second. I'll check how long it is," Kyle responded. He drew his sniper and peered out the window to see what was happening outside. He observed a massive group and instantly exclaimed, "We can't go through here, John," saying, "It's a full horde. If we walk through there, we're certainly dead."

He suddenly swung his car left into the forest and drove straight in; because it was the forest, the road was strewn with gravel and branches, Making driving more difficult; John managed to keep it all going until his eyes dazzled. The incredible memories of his daughter Sally, his wife, began to flood in, causing him to lose consciousness and have his eyes roll back......

"John? John? Where are we heading?" Ruthven inquired. "What's the matter with you, John? "..

"What's the problem, Ruthven?" Kyle placed himself in front of John, and when he watched him lose consciousness, Mike became concerned and terrified. He still recalled the day he discovered his father lying on the street while he was with his friends, and it appeared that John wasn't the only one having such memories...

"JOHN! WAKE UP- Kyle interrupted Ruthven, saying, "I'll hold John back, and you take charge of the wheel."

Ruthven attempted slapping him, but it had no effect as he was unconscious and unable to pay attention to what was happening. Mike and Anna were just apprehensive. Ruthven immediately seized control of the steering wheel and began making erratic turns.

It was difficult since he couldn't regulate his speed because John's feet were also locked there. Ruthven took a sharp curve, causing him to collide with a large tree and become stranded.......

"Is it stuck?" Anna inquired.

"It seems to be. Damn it, John," Ruthven remarked. "Everyone get out of the car," Ruthven said. "Hey Kyle, come help me get John out of this stupid car."

They dragged him out and tried to rouse him. Kyle poured some water on his head, which caused him to open his eyelids slightly....

"Oh, you've finally decided to wake up," Ruthven said, greatly relieved......

"What's going on?"....

"Well, Ruthven crashed the car," Kyle observed as he examined the damage......

"It was because John decided he wanted to snooze in between," Ruthven said shortly "I mean, what happened to you, John?" Ruthven inquired

Kyle quickly stopped Ruthven and stated, "Stop blaming him. It's not his fault."

" To be honest, I don't remember, but I saw someone in uhh, never mind, is Mike, okay?" John answered...

"All right, let's just try to fix the car and- Kyle abruptly stopped John, saying, "JOHN! The car is in no condition to be repaired."

Ruthven was watching this, but suddenly his mind was drawn to a voice. "Sorry to interrupt, but did you hear something?" Ruthven was perplexed.

They all became silent for a second as one twig broke, and Mike was ignorant of what was happening.

During that time, Kyle snatched Mike back, and they discovered the infected, but they were connected to something.

"Does that look like a tree?" Is the infection extending? How is it even possible?" Kyle was startled........

"It's known as a nest. The nest is where this infected grow stronger," Ruthven added, "You may argue the spot where I smashed the car is not a tree."

John saw that and decided to attack them using his gun, but he was suddenly stopped by Ruthven, who explained, "These growing infected, you may say, are more violent than others we have seen back there, first- they don't die with just a few bullets, second- they blow up when they die, and if someone comes in contact with them while they die, it spreads the infection more, third- they can only die using fire."...

"How do you know all of these things?" Anna asked.

Ruthven grinned and promptly told everyone to help him eradicate the infected nest. They eventually agreed and attempted to locate something that may start a fire. Everyone began inspecting their baggage for anything that may spark a fire while Kyle, Mike, and Anna started searching the car. Fortunately, when examining the car's rear pockets, Kyle discovered some alcohol in an unsealed glass bottle. Ruthven swiftly grabbed that bottle and removed the top; he rapidly spilt the entire bottle over the car and ordered everyone to get out.

Everyone fled in different ways until Ruthven fired his gun on the car's gas tank, causing it to explode and ignite a massive fire. They all watched numerous types of infected burning and begging. After they died, everyone noticed the whole area was covered with some kind of purple substance, which Ruthven referred to as "infection", they all noticed this burning and decided that it was time to move. John started walking on the trail of their car from where they had come.

It was growing darker and darker, they hadn't found their way back, and it was difficult to notice close infected people, so every step they took was dangerous. They eliminated the few infected who got in their way and kept going......

"Are you confident that we're on the right track?" Kyle inquired......

"We're going where the map leads us," John responded to Kyle.

Kyle sighed and continued, but Mike was exhausted and sat down for a few seconds. Kyle saw him and immediately ordered him not to rest because it was getting dark and unsafe even to stop, and as he grabbed his hand, he observed a brilliant light. The light was approaching from behind, and he instantly alerted everyone, but they all looked puzzled; the light was becoming more assertive and brighter and appeared to be moving or approaching them....

"Are you sure it's just a light?" Ruthven inquired...

"It isn't! We must run!!" "It's not light," John said, adding, "It's a forest fire."

They all began running, which drove several infected to chase them because they were easily spotted while running. John noticed a few infected in front of him and quickly killed them. Kyle continued to slay the infected that followed them from behind. The dread of fire and the infected had them running for their lives. They kept running until Mike fell because an infection leapt on him. He swiftly jumped up, pulled a knife from his pocket, stabbed him in the head, and started racing with them. His terror and will to survive boosted his confidence. It was only a short time until they spotted the road and the end of the forest. John took the lead, cutting through one of the branches blocking the entry and swiftly making room for everyone. The person he cared the most about was Mike, and he was the first person he let walkthrough.

They came upon a little gas station with a broken light, but it was preferable to spend the night there than running.

FIVE

The Gas Station

They all started walking to the gas station. John enlisted the help of others and silently slaughtered all of the infected that were outside. When he opened the door, an infected jumped on him, but Kyle soon saved him. They all eventually walked inside. There were a few infected inside, which they effortlessly killed, and they found a sign on the entrance that said, "STAY AWAY." They didn't think much of the warning since they felt much safer than before and relaxed a little on the floor. All of them were resting, except Mike and Anna, who were outdoors, which was also safe because there were no infected roaming around and there was adequate light to detect any infected approaching them.

They were chatting outside the gas station when Anna asked Mike, "Do you have any siblings?" Mike looked Anna in the eyes and told her, "I used to have a sister."....

"What?" Anna was confused and said, "What happened to her?"

Mike's heart was touched; it had been a long time since someone had asked him about his sister; he became emotional and hastily sought to dismiss the conversation by adding, "Can we please not talk about her!"

All the memories began to rush in, and Mike felt imprisoned in a dream that was no more an extended reality. Anna understood in some ways how Mike was feeling, so she rejected the conversation but asked him one final question......

"If it's all right with you, what was her name?"

"Sally"

When Mike rose and walked inside, the chat ended, leaving Anna alone, although she appeared happy with her company. It didn't last long; while she sat alone, she heard a loud bang from within, which startled her. She dashed inside to find out what was causing the noise and realized that the banging was coming from the same door that said: "STAY AWAY."

Mike was the first to hear the bang; Anna asked Mike whether they should go inside, but Mike instantly objected, suggesting that they keep away, but Anna was not of that mind; she told Mike that she would go in there to investigate what was going on. Mike protested once again and sought to warn Anna that "it's dangerous."

She tried to unlock the door, which was jammed due to a stick in the way. She eventually removed the lock and stepped in, but as she walked a few feet forward, she disclosed her gun strap and rolled a pistol out of it. She indicated that she always carries a gun for her safety. When she heard a noise, she took a few steps back. "Who's there?" she said immediately...

Mike overheard her and swiftly said, "Are you okay?"

Before she entered, her first thought was that a lone infected might have heard them while they were resting and were beating on the door, but it looked like this was a mistake.

She kept advancing; at this point, every step she took was perilous. She heard another noise, but this time she knew where it came from; her feet and pistol travelled in the same direction; with a vital aim, she walked forwards and froze when she reached the noise source. She investigated the empty blue barrels because she was suspicious, and when she found nothing, she moved in the opposite direction. Her feet began to shake slightly, but her aim remained solid and firm.

She examined the second barrel, but an infected jumped on her. She struggled for a few moments before killing the infected with her gun. The gunshot woke everyone up, and they looked at one other for a few minutes, puzzled, before rushing to the door that Anna had unlocked. When John observed Mike standing inside, he wanted to go as close to him as possible to ask whether he was alright. Anna was terrified yet also proud of herself. This happiness did not last very long, as she wasn't the only human in the room. She was immediately grabbed by a random person who appeared to be the cause of the bang, not the infected Anna had just slain. The survivor gripped Anna's mouth to keep her silent, but she was lucky since John and everyone had already arrived to help her....

"Who do you think you are?" While aiming his rifle towards the survivor's head, John inquired.

When the survivor saw the entire group holding him at gunpoint, he instinctively gripped Anna's hand…

"Don't shoot! Don't shoot! "I am a human." John interrupted the survivor immediately. "What were you doing inside?" John inquired....

"There were groups of survivors who put me in there. Where are they? Who are you?" The survivor said "Well, what the hell did you do that they had to put you in there?" Ruthven asked.

"That is not the issue. These people come every day and will come back tomorrow." Survivor said. "All of you should be wary because if these men notice you, they will fire without hesitation, "...

"We'll make sure that doesn't happen," John said. "You can now let go of her hand."

John told the survivor to stay precisely where he was and asked him one more question, "What time do they come in?"

The survivor turned to face John and told him. "Usually between 7 and 8."

John nodded and asked Ruthven to examine whether he was carrying firearms. He then told everyone to get enough rest today and to be ready for tomorrow. The following day, they created a plan to kill the survivors who would join them in the daytime. They considered baiting them with the person they discovered late at night. Kyle was atop the gas station while John and Ruthven covered from the front. Behind them came Anna, her mother, and Mike. One of the cars drew up to the gas station, and John instructed the survivor from behind to go out and distract them, so he did just that.

"YOU'RE ALIVE?"

The survivor broke out laughing, and behind him came other guys. One of them was a woman standing on top of the car with a large rifle ready to fire. They began a chat, during which Anna and Mike crept up behind them and took out two of the men there. The tables were rapidly turned. The man in the front saw them from the car mirror and shot Mike in the leg, while another seized Anna and forced her to toss the weapon. When John heard the shooting, he quickly turned around; Mike was in pain, and John ran down without hesitating.

Since the leader and the entire crew knew that others were with the survivor, he yelled, "You all may come out now!" and began packing to leave.

He laughed while he grabbed Anna and Mike, and threw them in their car, and rushed to go as fast as possible. John and everyone started racing, but he couldn't get there in time, and the mother burst into sobs....

"What are you looking at? We should chase them down!" John raged at Kyle upon seeing the mother in tears.

Kyle said it was unrealistic, considering they do not have a car. John wasn't having it, so he ran the entire distance, slaying any infected that got in his way. Seeing him, Ruthven decided to do just that, so he followed John. They both ran on the same path. The car was still visible, so they tried to burst the tires but were unsuccessful.

The vehicle continued till one of the tires busted open, Kyle went forward with a sniper, and John and Ruthven knew it was Kyle. The survivors were having none of it; there were four vehicles, and the car they shot was the last in line so they couldn't help Mike or Anna; there were just a few survivors who fought back, and the other three cars drove away. Those few survivors held John and his crew at bay, but John eventually defeated them. When John gained control, he swiftly held them up and interrogated them about their crew...

"I won't repeat it, but where were you going?!"

The survivors kept their mouths shut, and John tried and failed to get any information he could, concluding that they were better off dead. Those three cars immediately slowed down unexpectedly. The leader was not having it and yelled, "What's going on?"

He asked again but received no response; he got out only to discover that they had been set up by another group ahead of them. The leader immediately ordered the snipers to prepare. His crew had already assembled and were positioned in the foreground. The leader hurriedly took Anna and rushed into the burnt forest for protection, leaving Mike in the car, weeping in pain and trying to wrap a cloth around his leg....

"Hey, can you open these?" Anna asked but was quickly silenced by the leader, who said, "Hey, cut it out."

"You can't kill them all. You're low on the force," Anna explained.......

"Ha-ha, good one, you're a girl. You won't be able to handle it anyway," the leader joked.

He held a sniper and was hiding behind a fallen tree, which both hampered them and gave them a clear shot. He put on the scope and killed one of the ambushers. Unfortunately, his team kept dying, and he came to the point when the entire road was covered with his crew's corpses, leaving him with no choice but to accept Anna's assistance. So, the leader begged Anna for help and opened her. Anna didn't hesitate to take the gun from the leader's strap and shoot him in the head. She later realized that she was alone and had many people ahead of her to kill; if she didn't, she would die. "I didn't think this through," Anna said as she sensed footsteps coming from behind her. She whirled around hastily and aimed her revolver. Fortunately, John helped her feel more at ease, although the struggle was far from done. "How are you feeling?" Ruthven said from behind, which gave Anna confidence and optimism that she could kill the survivors....

"Where is Mike?" John instantly questioned Anna. "He's in the back of the car," Anna said...

"John, we should first focus on killing them," Kyle stated. When Anna understood that everyone was rooting for her, she decided to kill the survivors.

While talking, the ambushers were too eager and threw a grenade ahead of Anna. John and his team abruptly broke the small chat when they all saw the grenade right in front of them. The grenade was so close that they had no option but to leap out and be slightly damaged. This gave the ambushers a fitting conclusion...

"On your knees and hands up," the ambushers' commander said.

The explosion had just burst, and John's crew members were blinded. Anna began slowly hearing the ambushers' commands, and when she opened her eyes and saw every one of hers lying down, powerless, she knew it was over......

"Don't shoot don't shoot!" Kyle implored, looking down and holding his hands up....

"How many people are with you?" said the ambushers' crew leader....

"Only us! WE NEED YOUR HELP NOW!" As he requested their help, John stated

Mike began groaning louder and louder as he was in great agony. The ambushers were quickly attracted by Mike's attention and immediately unlocked the car's rear door and pulled Mike out. John was relieved to see Mike was still alive, but one thing troubled him: Mike was in a lot of pain, which would make it impossible for Mike to accompany them. They promptly grabbed Mike and urged John and his team to follow them. Mike had passed out and was lying on the vehicle's little seat.

The group was going strong, effortlessly removing all the infected who got in their way....

"Hurry, hurry, hurry."

The team was promptly stopped by one of the survivors guarding the gate. He attempted to take everyone out but was swiftly dismissed by one of their members, who said, "There's an emergency. Let us through." The survivor guarding the gate understood and instantly opened it without hesitation, taking Mike and fleeing in one of their tents labelled "EMERGENCY PURPOSES." When John and his team arrived and saw the tent, they had put Mike in, he hurried inside and found Mike lying on a bed as several nurses cleaned his wound. The group's commander abruptly interrupted John, "You shouldn't be worried. He'll be OK," she informed. John gave her a fleeting glance before nodding.......

"Take your time, then meet me in tent number one with your team," she added.

John stayed there in silence for a while before emerging and finding Kyle, Ruthven, Anna and her mother waiting for him.......

"Is everything all right?" Kyle inquired....

"Is Mike all right?" Anna pursued the inquiry.

After awkward seconds of stillness, John said, "YES." Before departing, he told them to come into tent number one.

They all entered the tent simultaneously, discovering a giant map and a miniature of the entire location. The leader told them to follow her before vanishing into another connected tent. They all followed her and saw many firearms and ammo, surprised to find so many weapons in such a tiny space....

"We do not help any random survivors we discover," the commander said, "but if we do, consider yourself lucky."....

"What do you expect in exchange?" John inquired solemnly......

"Wonderful, we need you to accomplish this." The leader finished by showing them the entire map and describing the strategy....

"A large structure stands at the far end of this city. It's known as the "SKALES," owned by a large survivor group. We will supply you with every bit of gun ammo you need as long as you deliver the leader to us ALIVE."......

"What's the snag?" John inquired...
"There is no catch," the leader stated thoughtfully...
"I'm not a moron; there's always a catch," John responded......
"There are none!"

When the discussion heated, John questioned the leader, "So, how come you've never captured him? Have you tried, or are you afraid, as I assume?"

The leader was undoubtedly outraged, but she quickly calmed herself down and stated, "We have tried a lot, but whoever has been there has not returned, and we are becoming smaller and smaller; we need more people to capture the city. They have blocked the entire city," she said, "or you might say they have changed the face of the city."......

"Wait, what exactly do you mean?" John stepped in. "The city has transformed into something else; they have clubs, casinos, music, and whatnot; you could say they have constructed their little theme park." The leader responded......

"How many people live there?" John inquired. "Hundreds, thousands, we don't know." the commander added. "It's a difficult task, but I can tell you that you will be rewarded."....

"We need some space to talk." As he went out of the tent, John remarked....

"WE HAVE NO TIME!" The leader responded by yelling back at John. After hearing the leader, John swaggered in and stated, "If you need help, you'll have to wait."......

"The tent beyond this will be your refuge for the night," the leader said with a kind gaze as she walked out. The sun had set and the night clouds had risen, but John couldn't sleep since he was battling with flashbacks about his daughter Sally. Seeing his kid almost die made him question his own life choices, but he didn't crumble; he was still confident.

When Ruthven noticed John awake, he approached him and said, "Is there something bothering you?"

John let out a little gasp and looked into the beginnings. Mike was awake and looking at the stars in the other tent.......

"I'm totally fine." John responded...

"I believe we should say yes," Ruthven said, "this is a terrific bargain, we're already low on ammo, and Mike needs support as well, we should take it John."

SIX

The Nine Floors Of Death

The city's highest building stood in the center. A classic white building that appeared to have never been touched by an infected remained unscathed. John was the first to leave the tent and found the leader near the food area. She was handing the meals to the older adults who had stayed. When John discovered Mike waiting at the back of the line, he was overjoyed. Mike was walking with a cane when John approached him and hugged him. "Are you all right, Mike?" He asked "How are you feeling?"....

"I'm OK," Mike replied with a smile while the leader came over to John and whispered in his ear, quickly telling Mike he would be back because he had something important going on. Mike nodded and strolled ahead to grab his meal; on the other hand, John began going with the leader. Ruthven emerged from the tent, followed by Kyle, and the others collected as they followed the leader. Everyone accompanied her to one of the rooms labelled "AMMUNITION." As soon as they walked in, they were all given different sorts of weaponry based on their preferences and abilities....

"Here, you'll have everything you need to fight and thrive," the leader promised.

While inspecting the weapons, John asked the leader her name, to which she answered, "Sierra."

"Well, Sierra, how long have you been preparing to capture the tower's leader and maybe destroy his tower?" John inquired......

"A few months have passed, and we have made numerous attempts, but we've always been unsuccessful in clearing the first part of this city, THE CASINOS," Sierra said.......

"I'll happily explain, but first, I need to prepare you for the mission properly," Sierra said

She showed them a variety of firearms and let them select whatever ones they felt most comfortable with. She started by pulling out heavy snipers, which she insisted on retaining since she knew they'd come in handy later.

"Who wants this beauty?" she inquired, pulling out one of her best snipers. "This beauty possesses the effective-

"The greatest effective range would be 460 meters/maximum effective range with a 3-9 scope of 900 yards and a maximum range of 3,725 meters." Kyle interrupted Sierra and stated

John grinned and looked at Kyle, who smirked and said it would be him. Sierra gave the rifle to Kyle, telling him, "Make every shot count."...

Kyle chuckled confidently and said, "I never miss."

Sierra then introduced the assault rifles and ammo package. "Who wants this precious item?" Sierra inquired.......

"I'll take it," John said....

"M4 Caliber-"...Kyle added, "The M4 Caliber, 30 rounds, employs 5.56 mm and has a rate of fire of 700-950 shots/min cyclic."

"Are you finished?" Sierra expressed her rage..."Sierra cut it," John said.

She pulled out the minigun, which she gave Ruthven because he was the only one who understood how to handle heavy weaponry, leaving Anna and her mother without any.......

"The M134 minigun fires 7.62 mm rounds-.

"Sorry for the interruption, but-...

"WHAT?" Sierra said in frustration

"Don't you think this is a little heavy for me?" Ruthven inquired solemnly......

"Yes, we know; that's why we'll hide it in one of our cars as part of our plan, and you'll be in charge of this thing?" Sierra stated.

Ruthven accepted calmly and waited for Sierra to carry out her plan......

"We're almost there; the only thing we're lacking is- "Armors", Kyle interrupted....

"DO YOU HAVE ANY PROBLEM?" Sierra grabbed her gun on Kyle and aimed right at his head. Kyle wasn't easily afraid. Therefore, he pointed his gun back. John also pulled out his gun and aimed at Sierra...

"DO YOU ALSO?" Sierra told John..."Me too, ma'am," Ruthven said, reaching for his gun and drawing it before her.... "Lower your rifle, SIERRA; fighting among ourselves is pointless; we have a lot of work to do," John stated

"Take the armor kits immediately and let's get ready," Sierra said. "Meet me on the other side after you've finished getting ready. We have a plan that we want to carry out."......

"So what about me?" Anna inquired...."Come with me, you and your mother," Sierra said as she gently lowered her rifle and looked at John and his crew, who were still pointing sharply at her. She went out with Anna and her mother, leaving John and his team to get ready in the tent.

Sierra led Anna to one of the many tents, where she requested her mother to allow her and Anna some time, to which her mother consented and sat on one of the benches outside the tent area. she brought a tiny box and opened it in front of Anna. There were several knives and quiet handguns. They also included gun holders and gloves. Because there were no vast firearms, Anna wondered, "What about big guns as they all use?"

"Why do you require those?" Sierra was perplexed and questioned Anna......

"Are you serious? They're rather large and powerful," Anna said......

"No, I mean, why do you need those when you're so skilled at sneaking up on them and killing them silently?" Sierra inquired......

"It's simply a lot better and more enjoyable," Anna said, excited to handle the hefty weaponry... "It's not a good time here, Anna. We have a severe problem, and I can't afford to screw up my plan. We need your help." Sierra said...."All right, what's the plan?" Anna inquired in a dull tone.......

"First, take what you need, then wait for my arrival," Sierra remarked while delivering Anna the essential equipment. Anna began to put on her armor and fill herself with bravery. She selected a couple of knives that she was familiar with and armed herself with the silent handguns. She then went back into the previous room and found everyone.

They were all clutching their firearms, indicating they were all prepared and serious about the plan. Sierra finally entered the room. She wiped off the table before them and placed a map on it. "If you have any questions, please ask them right away. We don't have much time, so pay attention." Sierra said "Now, here's the map"........

"Take a good look," Sierra said....

"What exactly is this? Do you see how massive it is? How are we supposed to go in? It's a death trap." Ruthven stated....

"Scared already?"

"He's correct. Look into it, and it's a trap. It's a whole dead ass city. It's virtually difficult even to get in," John said as he placed his hand on the map and made eye contact with Sierra......

"I know this, but I have a solution-...

"You have nothing. It's impossible. Forget it," Ruthven remarked......

."Well, what else are you going to do?" Sierra said, "We'll figure it out," Ruthven added....

"The entire city is under his control, and you can't go back because Mike still needs medical attention, and he's in our hands," Sierra said

John had seen enough of this today, but after listening to all Sierra had just said, he would not sit quietly. The rifles were drawn once more, but Anna was also the one to pull the gun this time. "Don't you dare now? It's not his fault, don't pull him into this," she added.

The other survivors arrived and swiftly drew their firearms at them, ordering John and his crew to drop their guns......

"WOULD YOU PLEASE LEAVE BEFORE WE SHED ANY BLOOD?" The survivor was in authority.

Ruthven threw his gun on the floor, where Kyle calmly collected it and placed it on the table, whereas John handed the rifle to Sierra and began heading out with his crew.......

"Anna, we recommend you and your mother stay with us." Sierra insistent......

"No, you've done enough for today," Anna responded; she and John walked outside. The gate was opened for them, and as they stepped beyond, Anna's mother approached her and asked, "WHERE ARE YOU GOING?" Anna remained mute as she slowly walked away, leaving her behind; the gates were shut, and they were all gone, leaving the mother alone...

"What exactly is going on? She's your mother!" John said to Anna. "Go back!"....

"She's not- Anna began walking in front of John, Kyle, and Ruthven, who followed her and continued questioning her, "What do you mean by that?"

When John mysteriously came to a halt, he raced back to them and began beating on the door. Three of them followed John back. Sierra answered the door and met him with a weapon pointed at him. "What do you want?" she questioned.

"You know why I'm here," John said, looking at her. Sierra stared dead in John's eyes and decided to throw Mike out. She instructed her men to bring Mike and toss him out, despite the fact that all of his wounds were nearly healed.

Sierra whispered, "You have till tomorrow morning to decide, and he will stay with me until then."

The doors were shut, and John was at his level; he continued firing the door until he was caught from behind by Ruthven; he attempted to calm John down but was ineffective until he dragged him out...

"Well, here we are. I thought I'd never see this place again," Ruthven stated as they returned to the gas station. They all threw their belongings on the ground, and John was looking for something in his rucksack when he was approached by Anna, who told him, "We have to get medical treatment for Mike."....

"I understand, but how?" John inquired...

"We must accept what they say. That's all ". Anna responded to John with a solemn expression on her face.......

"We've been through this before, Anna; it's a death trap. Why are you here?" John inquired. "Anna? It seems like you knew Sierra from someplace. "..

"She knew my father, but I'd rather be with someone I trust," Anna responded......

"So you joined us," John responded....

"I spoke with Mike that night, and he told me you had a daughter," Anna explained.

John paused momentarily before looking at Anna and said, "It's the past, don't worry about it?"

Anna was skeptical, saying, "I assumed you wanted a daughter more than anything at this moment. "She continued, "My mother died when I was small, and the one who was with me was my mom's betrothed friend. I didn't know her much and wouldn't say I liked living with her; honestly, she never cared about me. Growing up with her was a mess, and she made hell.

I have always wanted to escape, but I failed every time I tried, so I thought maybe it was time to make my own decisions. I don't know you much, but I'm sure I'll be a great sibling to Mike and the great daughter you have always wanted, just like Sally.

"JOHNNNN!!!!!!!!! Wait! Follow me, Anna." John spoke up fast. They could hear sounds outside. Ruthven approached the windows to look, but they were entirely covered by dead plants that had grown since they had been ignored for years, and he couldn't see anything....

"Stay on foot," John instructed, handing Anna a tiny gun he had prepared for an eventuality as if he had begun to trust her......

"On it, you guys," Ruthven said as John and Kyle grabbed the lead and headed outdoors, but they couldn't find a human. Kyle joined him from behind, but there was no one, not a single trace. A man clothed entirely in while and green dashed in from the side. He used bolas to assault Kyle's leg, causing him to collapse. John instantly noticed him and attempted to shoot.

He levelled the gun at his head, and the guy dived down and attacked his gun hand with staff before hitting. John groaned. The man chained both of them and began questioning them....

"What's the matter with this guy?" Kyle said...

"Hey! Over here, I only ask questions.".
"What do you want? Bullets, food?" remarked John

He was holding a pistol to their heads when a round was fired at his gunpoint, causing him to drop his weapon. When Ruthven and Anna emerged, Ruthven attacked him while holding his revolver. "Are you okay?" Anna questioned John as she raced up to him.

After a minute, the guy was tied, and John and Kyle stood before him.... "Now we're the ones asking the questions," John stated as he held the man at gunpoint. "Can you tell me your name?" John inquired....

"Da-," David"......

"David, huh," John remarked, smirking. "How old are you?" John asked....

"I'm 19," David responded....

"What are you doing all by yourself?" Kyle inquired. "I was running away from something," Davis explained. "From whom?" John inquired....

"A survival group-

Suddenly At that point, there was a massive outcry. It appeared that survivors were ambushing them; everyone heard the gunshots and sought for safety as quickly as they could. David was instantly stopped, but the firing continued, and the cars ran close to their gas station. When they heard survivors approaching, they pulled David inside and shut the door. David proposed releasing him and offering to assist them.

Because John didn't like the notion, he went alone and tried slaughtering the survivors. He decided to go up on the roof to have a better view. Ruthven and Kyle led the way. John pulled out his rifle and began counting the survivors and their weapons....

"Do not kill," David urged.

He exited and told Ruthven and Kyle not to shoot. "How on earth did you get out?" Ruthven inquired. "Now isn't the time to ask," David said.

John was still on the upper end. He shot the bullet near a survivor, signaling that they should go, but the survivors were not pleased and began firing at the gas station. During this gunfight, Ruthven and Kyle were spotted and were being shot....

"What should we do about these guys?" Ruthven said. John was also being extensively shot at and was, therefore, unable to attack.

David jumped on the chance and exited the gas station. Rather than bolting, he yelled, "STOP GUYS, THEY ARE FRIENDLY!"

All of the survivors appeared to recognize David and came to a standstill. "What on earth are you doing here?"......

"I was lost," David said. Everyone, including John, survived. "Who exactly are they?" John inquired. "What are your thoughts? We are the Red Hawks." "My name is Rack, and I am the Red Hawks' leader." "My name is John."

"Hey, can I talk to you for a minute?" David approached him as Rack stated.

David and Rack were both standing far away from John, and Rack questioned David about him. John discreetly asked Ruthven how David had escaped, and Ruthven answered that he, too, was curious..."David, what are we doing here?" Rack inquired.
"These men might be able to help us," David said... "We don't need new members; what's the big deal about them?" Rack inquired....
"They know how to kill and I saw them exit the military quarantine zone. They were able to flee just like us," Davis added. He and Rack returned and invited them to accompany them......
"Come with us."

"How come we believe you?" John responded.

John was skeptical of him until he recalled Mike and Anna....... "Are you sure you don't need any help?" Rack inquired. "There is one exception," John responded...

"What are you doing, John?" Ruthven stated... "Can you help us? We want to pass that city," John inquired.

Rack and David were experiencing ambivalent feelings and remained silent. When John didn't get them, he inquired again, and Rack explained that the city is guarded by an organization called Human Hunters. "They shoot everyone who arrives from another city, and you are not permitted to cross the city without their permission."....

"Who is in charge of this group?" John inquired..."He was a four-star senior commander in the army named Adrien Hart." Rack responded, "Those guys are tough."......

"Is there a ... way of getting away?" John inquired... "No, but he does have a brother named Aiden Hart. He might be able to help you." Rack responded... "Can you tell us where we can get him?" John inquired. "It's not the right time. Come with us, rest, and we'll all go in the morning." Rack said

John was not pleased with the plan, but he had no option. They wanted to cross that city, so they followed them. When they arrived, they all slept. They were each given a bed to relax in. John still didn't believe rack, so he got out of bed and came out of his camp, where he spotted Rack. He approached him and chatted about his plans for the day. "What forces you to help us?" John inquired.......

"We presume you are all from the quarantined military area," Rack said......

"You were there?" In disbelief, John inquired... "We were, and we want to go through that city as well," Rack said......

"But where are you going?" John inquired...

"The Unmarked," David explained.

John was stunned and kept prolonged eye contact. He recognized what he was addressing and instinctively questioned, "How do you know about that?" David laughed, blurting, "The guy who told you, Look, we're working toward the same objective. We all play as a team until we achieve our objective. Then, we break up."

They were a small group living in an abandoned camp where only they could live. John shrugged and questioned about their morning plans.... "We decided to leave at six o'clock, and boom, bang," Rack responded, chuckling.

John returned Rack's grin and departed the conversation. John returned to his bed and attempted to sleep, but he could not since he was again greeted by his floating memories of his daughter and wife. Time passed, and they departed the following day. John and his crew had been allocated their car and followed them. They drove them to a little town close to where they were staying. There were closed stores and schools. "So, where are we? Surprisingly, I've never been here before." Ruthven stated

They were led to an old school and told to proceed from there. They exited their truck and entered. The school appeared to be deserted. They were anticipating infected people but have yet to come across any...

"Where does he live, Aiden Hart?" John inquired.

"Just a few blocks from this school," David responded. They reached the end of school. However, the door was shut. They attempted to enter through a second door, which was also blocked. They discovered that all of the entries were either blocked or jammed....

"Do we have another option?" Ruthven inquired. "Through the cellar." Rack responded...

"It could be worse." Ruthven stated....

"Believe me, it is." Rack stated quietly...

They all took the cellar walkway, which was completely saturated with water and contaminated with dead bodies. "Did anyone pass by here?" John inquired. "Not from my end." Rack said

When John approached one of the dead infected, he discovered that he had recently died. He yelled and warned everyone to be alert, but just as he finished, a wave of survivors appeared behind them. Everyone rushed to hide, but Rack was shot before he could budge.......

"Rack! ARE YOU OKAYYYYY" The remaining survivors took cover too...."DAVID! Take cover, or you'll end up dead like him". When John indicated that David had found cover, they all began firing. There were a few survivors who have been wounded, but there were a lot of them. The survivors were getting closer, and John's or Rack's crews were running low on manpower.

John realized that if they didn't do something, they'd be better off dead, so he tried to sneak behind them. He dropped down from his position and began going through old boxes that were not strong and were dispersed over the area; a single man could easily shoot him via the boxes. After going for a few seconds, John realized he was barely halfway there, so he went through the iron shelf. He was overly vulnerable because there weren't many items to cover or completely conceal him.... "Get moving!" John said quietly.

Ruthven spotted one of the survivors coming across John's side, so he jeopardized his life by eliminating him and exposing himself.

All survivors abruptly stopped firing and began rushing via the opposite exit. "What's going on?" Ruthven inquired.

Suddenly, the floor began to move, and all of the racks and boxes began to move, revealing John through the other side; fortunately, the survivors were fleeing and did not notice John.......

"What in the world is going on?" David inquired. "Maybe an earthquake," Kyle answered....

"It's not possible." David said....

"It's the end of the world, everything is possible." Kyle said......

"BEHIND YOU, KYLE!!" John yelled

Hundreds of infected were pouring through the narrow entry, quickly covering the whole area before entering the main basement. "RUN, INFECTEDS!" Ruthven stated as David attempted to shoot them but was quickly stopped by Kyle "It's not worth it to kill them, Run!"

While still hiding among the shelves, John came across some infected, but they did not attack him. He understood that the infected that had come through couldn't see him. John was perplexed since he had never seen anything like that before. They were only able to hear noises. John took advantage of the situation and tossed a stone in the other direction of his enemy. The infected followed the stone, as John went the opposite way........

"That was really close." John stated

He began rushing after blocking the door with a shelf. Ruthven and his crew mates were doing the same, blocking the door behind them. John was following in their tracks in order to catch up with them.

He attempted to open the door, but it was barred from the other side by Ruthven, who was unaware that John was trapped on the other side due to him. "No!" John stated

When Ruthven and his companions walked from the school, they discovered that the same group they had encountered inside was waiting for them outside at gunpoint. They were surrounded and had no choice but to fight. "Aiden, it is David, don't shoot." David said as he fortunately, observed that the survivors who assaulted them were Aiden Hart's men, but he failed to recognize them due to the dim lighting in the cellar. "Lower your gun, he's one of us," Aiden Hart said. "What are you doing here, and who are these people?" He inquired......

"They're with me, and we wanted to see you," David said.......

"Where has Rack gone?" Aiden Hart inquired...
"He's ou-out for an errand. He'll be back." David replied.......

"Huh, let's get you all to safety; there are a lot of infected around here." Aiden Hart said. .
"Davis, John is missing!" Ruthven stated. "What? Was he not following us?" Davis expressed his astonishment......

"I'm not sure!" Ruthven responded....

"Aiden, one of our guys is still in there and needs help." David said......

"OK, everyone, let's go in." Aiden Hart was in command. They all barged in through the door and began searching for John. They divided into two groups and began their search for him. When John noticed an infected approaching him, he pulled out his gun and shot the infected in the head. More infected ones were drawn in by the gunshots.

"Oh, Shit I obviously did not think things through "John expressed sorrow in his tone. Ruthven and Kyle heard the gunfire and followed the sound, expected John to be nearby......

"Everyone, this way!" Ruthven stated

They pursued him till they came to a room full of infected people with no other way out. They searched silently for John but were unable to locate him because the entire area was contaminated and blocked all access routes. "We can get rid of them." According to Aiden Hart......

"We can't do it. We must find another way. This room is crawling with infected. We'll merely draw more people." David said....

"We'll search for another option. David, and you two, please come with me." Aiden Hart stated this while pointing to Ruthven and Kyle. Anna remained silent and began moving on her own to see deeper...

"Just stay here, and we'll try to look further." David said. They took a couple steps forward and took shelter. They tried to get a closer look at what the infected were drawn to and constructing a circle around something. "Did you see anything?" Aiden Hart inquired...

"No, my view is blocked." David responded... A gunshot was fired out of the blue. "There's a bullet!" "Stay put."......

"It's got to be John." Kyle said

"How do you know?" Ruthven stated as the infected were blocking the Door, suddenly the door shattered..."Come on, let's get moving." Aiden stated

Aiden and David began to move. Kyle noticed them and they began to follow them into the door. They noticed a whole room full of infected people.

It was a large hall with several entrances. They noticed one of the doors open and figured John had gone through it. "OK, let's go through that door." They dashed past that door and emerged, noticing John running at the end of the corridor.

They tried calling him but stopped when they noticed a swarm of infected racing after him... "Keep your voice down," Aiden advised. They rapidly began sprinting across the corridor, suddenly the doors of the interconnected corridor began to breach as well as the infected swarmed from all sides. "Hell, we have to retreat." Aiden stated......

"And what about John?" Ruthven inquired, perplexedly. "We can't get through here, but follow me; I know a way he could have gone." Aiden stated.

They took off sprinting up the stairs. Ruthven and Kyle were standing at the back. They began firing the infected and continued on their way. They got to the top and realized that there was no way out.... "What should we do now?" Ruthven asked...

"We jump." Aiden stated.

"Are you insane?" Kyle said....

"Well, if you want to die from an infected person, by all means do so." Aiden stated......

"There is no other option, Kyle." Ruthven stated…
"All right, let's get going." Kyle said

The infected ultimately smashed and unlocked the door they had barred behind them. They all jumped. Because all of the doors were locked, John was still trying to find a way out. He entered a room filled with infected people, and others followed him. He attempted to find a way out, but all the doors were blocked. He noticed an old rusted ladder leading to an iron platform above a basketball court. He had no choice but to ascend swiftly.

The entire horde of infected quickly flooded the entire area. Near him, John found some rags and booze. It seemed strange to see an alcoholic bottle in school, but time had gone and anything was imaginable.

He soon realized what he ought to do. He took the bottle and wrapped it in a cloth before lighting it on fire. He waited for the infected to congregate in a specific location, then he fired at a couple of them to attract others. The infected poured in, and the area was swamped by them, and more were attempting to get inside. When John tossed the bottle at the infected, the entire area started burning in matter of seconds.

John sat and watched his destruction. The infected were burning, and as he was seeing them. Kyle and Ruthven had left school at this point. "Is everyone okay?" Aiden stated.......

"Yeah, we're Fine." David said...."How are you two doing?" Aiden remarked to Kyle and Ruthven, offering them his hands to help them stand up. "We're OK." Kyle said....

"We should avoid this place since it is one of the most overcrowded infected nests," Aiden stated.... "We can't leave because we still have one of ours in there." Kyle said...

"Do you realize that if we go in, we will die horribly?" Aiden replied angrily......

"He's correct, going back in is too dangerous; we should find another route." David said....

"Listen, no offense, but I don't want my man to die because of one person." Aiden stated....

"What the hell are you doing?" Kyle stated as he pulled the gun from his pocket and aimed it towards Aiden..."HEY! STOP!" David offered that Ruthven and Kyle go there and save John alone if that's what they really needed as he stepped in between them and ordered them to stop arguing.

Aiden and his friends fled, leaving Ruthven and Kyle to rescue John. Kyle pushed his way through the fence and began looking for a way in.

They observed the fire that John had started and dashed towards it. "John! John! John!" Kyle yelled

They saw John through the smashed glass and attempted to reach him. When John spotted them, he requested for help......

"Break the window!"

The area was becoming increasingly heated, and more infected were fleeing. There was nowhere for John to run or hide as several infected began to emerge from the school, breaking all the windows and rushing outdoors. A couple of them spotted Kyle and Ruthven and instantly began chasing them....

"There aren't many; we can get rid of them." Ruthven stated......

"You go left, and I'll go right." Kyle said

When the infected struck the ground, they immediately began shooting and cleared their way, then they instantly focused on how to get John and figure out the best way into that can save Him. "Kyle, there's a broken window over there. It is connected to the tree. We might be able to get in and get John."...

"Alright".

Ruthven placed his foot down and gripped the branch as Kyle locked his hand. He rose and reached out his hand to Kyle. He instinctively grasped his hand and started climbing. The window was just next to John's.

After going in, they glanced at John and directed him to come to this side, but there was a large gap for John to leap over. "He needs something to reach for." Kyle said. "And fast, because it's becoming hot." John stated

They came upon a board and attempted to build a bridge with it. John took the plank from the opposite side, slid it between the two, and began walking on it. "Come on, John, it is working." Kyle said

Kyle extended his hand for John to grab, but the board snapped and dropped directly on the flaming infected. Fortunately, John grasped the platform's edge and was dragged by Kyle and Ruthven......

"Are you completely OK, John?" Kyle inquired... "Yeah, I'm functioning." John responded in hushed tones. "Well, let's get out of here before we turn into that flaming board or the burning infected." Ruthven stated......

"All right, let's go." John stated

They landed and carried on their journey. "Where has David gone?" John inquired....

"He, uh, left the building." Kyle responded. "We shouldn't have trust in them."

"Alright, but where is Anna?" John inquired.... Kyle's eyes widened when he realized, "Wasn't she with you?"

"NO! What the hell, we've got to get back in!" John gave the order and dashed inside. Kyle and Ruthven exchanged a cursory look before taking off after John.

John grabbed one of the infected and instantly flung him down to clear a path inside the school; it wasn't long before the class and other rooms caught fire as a result of the fire ignited by John. Because no one knew where Anna was, John began yelling her name. "John! Keep your calm!" Kyle insisted......

"What's the matter with you? Anna has gone missing, and-...

"YOU'RE MAKING NO PROGRESS! You're merely attracting more infected people". Kyle responded, "Perhaps you should have taken better care of her." After answering, John walked away...."He's right there, Kyle, let's go, someone is missing from our group." Ruthven stated

They all moved off to another corridor that led to several classrooms, Ruthven checking all the classrooms on the left and Kyle checking the classrooms here on right. Kyle attempted to unlock one of the doors that were barred from the outside; there was also a little note written, "KEEP OUT," but Kyle was in a haste and didn't see the piece of paper. John kept yelling Anna's name, he inspected all the classrooms but found no leads,

Therefore, he rushed madly towards one of the blazing halls and began clearing a few burning infected who were in his path. When Kyle entered the door, he was immediately jumped by an infected that was waiting inside. Ruthven noticed him and eventually shot the infected.......

"Are you OK, Kyle?" Ruthven stated

Kyle did not respond and began stepping into the room that he had just opened, only to discover that the entire class was vacant.

John entered one of the classes and, to his astonishment, found one of Anna's belongings, her rifle. He kept yelling her name, but this time Ruthven and Kyle heard the voice and raced towards him. Unfortunately for john, many infected people had also heard his call, and they all began racing toward him in no time. When Kyle and Ruthven arrived near John's class, they were met by infected on their route. They both tried to shoot them but were quickly outnumbered by the infected. All three shut the door and stood inside, watching the infected pounding and burning...

"What do we do now? We're stuck!" Ruthven stated and seemed bewildered

While they were all watching the infected, someone shot a couple of those from outside, and the infected immediately fled towards the person who fired it, leaving John, Kyle, and Ruthven unscathed with a clear way to go.

"That's her."

John hurried alone again and chased the infected; Ruthven and Kyle joined him; they all sprinted until they found John standing; there was a person standing just in front of John......

"It appears that we have found you." Aiden stated. "What in the world are you doing here?" Kyle stated in a hushed tone......

"John, whatever happens, don't put your trust in this person." Ruthven went on....

"I know what I said back then, I didn't want to jeopardize my group's lives because they had nothing to do with you except me, I never said I wouldn't help you, but it appears like you're alright to battle any infected," Aiden explained......

"You are totally unbelievable," Kyle responded... "NOT RIGHT NOW! David, do you remember the girl that was around us? We need to find her and I don't want any fights; if you want to help us, do so or go back." John stated as he began to ascend the steps...

"We both are heading down," Aiden said to Ruthven and Kyle, "you guys check all the other rooms, this school is acknowledged as one of the finest and largest schools in the city center, there are surely a lot of places you haven't looked into, I am sure."

"Better not tell us what to do!" Kyle responded in a frenzy as Aiden broke eye contact and followed David down the stairs. Ruthven and Kyle, on the other end, parted up and went their own ways. As john passed through the doors, He clutched his gun. Slowly, he kept opening the doors in front of him. He did see a few infected along the way, but he adopted a different strategy this time, walking discreetly while doing his utmost to not alert any infected as he pass through them. He luckily passed a couple of infected, however that wasn't the end of it; he discovered an enormous crater that had demolished the entire hallway and part of the classes; while he moved closer to the crater, one of the infected from behind caught him and began chasing him; John had no option but to jump down.

He relentlessly took out all the infected that had hopped in after him, but was soon stopped when he encountered a large number of infected running towards him, this time he began shooting them but also started to run in the opposite direction, he ultimately killed all the infected but then was instantaneously clashed with somebody, both of them had faced their backs and had no idea that the other person was heading straight at each other.......

"Who are you?!" Get the hell out of here, go go go go" Anna closed her eyes and began whimpering... "It's okay, baby, it's just me, it's just me-"

"It's alright it's okay in here now *Sally* everything is going to be okay," John instantly hugged her and tried to soothe her.

Sally?

Anna calmed herself and gently rose up with John's help.

"Should we go?" John stated Anna nodded and retrieved her gun. The sun was gradually setting, and the sky was turning orange. "Should we trust him?" Kyle said...... "What happened to you suddenly? We don't have another choice." John stated

John and his crew exited the school and resumed their trek; they were still with Aiden since, according to John, Aiden was their last chance of liberating Mike and crossing the city, but he didn't trust him..."We've arrived," Aiden remarked....

"What do you mean?" John was perplexed and inquired. "So, what exactly is this?"....

Kyle stated, "These are just burnt cars and trees. "... "It's not always what you see." Aiden stated...

"What do you mean?" John inquired....

"Don't make judgments too fast; it's what's underlying that counts." Aiden stated. "Come with me."

They followed Aiden through the wrecked cars. Just at bottom, they uncovered an old, burned-out automobile door.

Aiden pushed open the vehicle door, revealing an iron fence beneath. Everyone dropped down to uncover a large area packed in beds, guns, food, and lethal equipment, an ideal spot for survival. "Did you build these all by yourself?" John inquired....

"No, I have folks that live here." Aiden stated. "We are one of the first survivor groups to go through all of this and come out alive."

Aiden directed one of his men to make John and his group feel at ease here. "Come with me." They made their way inside and sat.

"Finally, a place to relax after such a long journey." Ruthven stated... "Remember, we have to cross the city." John stated

David entered their room and noticed that everyone was unwinding except for John, who had been standing upright with a solemn look on his face. "Aiden has invited you outside. I believe you should inform him about Adrien Hart." David said...

"Yeah, we'll be there," John answered, looking up. He then walks away from Ruthven and Kyle without mentioning anything. Kyle stares at him and asks Ruthven, "What's up with him?"....

"Not a clue," Ruthven remarked, perplexed.

Aiden was eating when he saw John coming in and immediately offered him some food. "We need to talk." As he took a little map from his luggage, John replied gravely.

"Why are you so serious?" Aiden stated. "Don't you like this place?"......

"Do you remember Adrien Hart?" John inquired as Aiden remained quiet for a couple seconds before changing his expression and ordering everyone to leave the room except David and John. Ruthven and Kyle stepped in and took seats next to John....

"He was my younger brother." Aiden stated... "We know where he is and we need your help." John replied......

"He was a great brother, among the greatest people I could have asked God for, I still remember when the apocalypse struck, all of it happened so quickly, within a matter of minutes the streets were encircled with all these infected people, I remember I was still back home chopping vegetables and Adrien was out with mother, she was a single mom, but then I also remember that the minute I turned on the news I understood something was going on, there were news anchors just babbling about some infection, as I watched the tape of the infection, I instantly called Adrien but he didn't answer however I kept calling him until I received a voice message, I immediately tapped it and got into my car because I was ready to drive and save them but then as I heard the voice note my heart missed a beat and I felt everything was over and I had lost in my life" Aiden continued,

"AIDENN!! MOTHER IS DEAD!! I HAVE NO IDEA WHAT IS GOING ON AHHHHHH!!!!!!!!! He was sobbing, and all the infected were chasing him or something, I'm not positive, my phone fell and-"

Aiden stumbled to a halt and sat in silence; everyone peered at Aiden with their heads down for a short moment until John said, "Hey, I see you and-". "AND?" Aiden interjected and smacked his hands on the table, shattering everything. "You have no idea what happened to me."

Anna became enraged. "You don't know what he's been through, HE LOST HALF OF HIS FAMILY, don't you dare-"....

"Anna! "It's OK," John said....

"It's difficult to accept, when you already know you've lost it all and there seems to be nobody on the other side to save you," Anna added as Aiden was staring at Anna until he turned his head gently towards John and said, "I'm sorry, brother."......

"No need," John said........

"John, you mentioned Adrien being alive; is that correct?" Aiden inquired......

"We believe we know where he is and need your help." Kyle stated as he sat on one of the chairs. Aiden instantly called one of his crew members and instructed him to alert everyone about the recent meeting in here. Everyone dashed forward, and the space was rapidly filled....

"I have fantastic news: my brother is still alive. These guys, John and his crew, located him. I haven't seen him in almost seven years. Tomorrow morning, we'll meet with John and his crew in the hopes of finding them a better place to live. We'll undoubtedly meet the best brother and a new member of our crew "Aiden stated

After the meeting, everyone exited the dining room, but John went directly to Aiden to address Sierra and her group, who meant to shoot and kill Adrien. "What makes her want to do that?" Aiden inquired...

"Adrien, she believes, is a horrible person and they will kill her and her crewmates sooner or later." John responded....

"It will not happen tomorrow. We'll get there just fine." Aiden said......

"All well, then." As he walked away, John went to follow up on Ruthven and Kyle. They were talking about something when they all heard a massive explosion and a lot of gun shots. They hastily exited their room and noticed everyone arming themselves with firearms and gear. Aiden noticed them and dashed towards them. "Lads, we're under attack, so get your firearms and everything you must to protect yourselves." Aiden stated......

"We have been under attacked!" inquired John. "Who are they?"......

"It's one of the surviving organizations. We were once a part of it, however they booted all of us out suddenly, so in rage, we executed their team leader and fled. They have been hunting for us ever since that day. I believe they found us today, so you must prepare immediately." Aiden stated.......

"Knock, knock Aiden, come out here and play." They broke down the door with their crew as Aiden and his crew began to seek cover....

"Don't hide, Aiden; we know you're here."

Aiden remained hidden, forcing the survivors to discover them themselves. The survivors fired shots through each of the facility's doors. They began to move. The surviving group saw one of Aiden's crew members and began advancing toward them.

John was hidden elsewhere, far off from Aiden's crew. He spotted the survivors making their way to one of Aiden's crew members. "STOP! Who are all of you? ". John bolted and blew his cover....

"What the heck is he doing?" Aiden wondered. Since David was close by, he said, "I don't know, something's up." The survivors set their sights on him, aborted their check, and asked John several questions...

"What happened to Aiden?"....

"Who are you?" John inquired....

"We ask questions around here."...

"What's your name?" John inquired once more, this time in a stern tone. "What's with the attitude? My name is Bart."......

"What exactly do you want?" John inquired...

"We're looking for Aiden, and you're going to tell me where he is." Bart responded....

"Oh, try me then, and we'll see how you get him." John stated as he dropped all of his weaponry and firearms. "No gun, no armor, one on one, fight like a real man," John confronted the survivor group's leader...

"WOO! You must expect to lose" Bart stated

Bart had a wonderful and muscular figure, yet he also looked menacing; the apocalypse had affected everyone differently. Bart instructed his men to lay down all firearms, and they did so.

John and Bart exchanged death stares. Nobody had touched each other yet, however Bart was the first to make a move, attempting to punch John but barely missing it. Bart continued striking John, and after a few punches, he was able to land a stiff jab on John. John collapsed, but instantly stood up and said nothing. "It seems that you need more." Bart stated...

They kept hustling and in between John landed some nice blows but then was regrettably knocked to the ground by Brat, all the survivors of Bart's crew began laughing out loud. But this was not the end.

John didn't give up, he continued rising right back and smacking him, and so this time he succeeded in making

Bart tumble down, as John stood right over him, saying nothing and starring dead in Bart's eyes. Bart became enraged and stood up as if nothing had occurred, much more so than before......

"I'm not done yet," John stated....

"Neither am I!" said Bart.

Bart charged up again and tried to throw a punch; John managed to deflect it but was eventually caught by Bart's strike. He suddenly grabbed Bart's leg and slammed him down, giving him a significant edge. Without hesitation, John continued to beat him in the face, however two of Bart's men restrained him and several men arrived afterwards.

Bart took some time to crawl up and attack John; the battle was no longer fair; John was being held by Bart's men and was constantly getting punched. When John got struck down, he struggled to keep his eyes open...

"LEAVE HIM ALONE!" Bart said. "I'll deal with him,"

John's face was splattered with blood and he didn't see a thing, Bart pulled a little knife from his vest, signaling that the battle wasn't really intended to be fair from the beginning.......

"Where the hell is Aiden now?" screamed Bart, holding the knife around his neck....

"ON YOUR DEATH BED"

Bart was shot, everything fell silent for a few moments…

"A- An- Anna," John stuttered.

Aiden's crew eventually exposed themselves and began shooting all the survivors who had entered. Anna promptly tried to carry John however he was in no condition to stand or walk, so Kyle reached out and helped her out....

"JOHN! Are you okay?" Aiden entered and stated. "You all should keep your mouths quiet, even though when John was being dragged up by those men and brutally beaten, right up until he was ready to be killed, you all NEVER CAME TO SAVE HIM!" Anna responded as she returned her attention to John.

Aiden and the others stood there, realizing that they had won the struggle against Bart but had lost something important.

John was still alive...."I'm OK," John responded as he stood up. "Just give me some time, I'm OK," John said.

They all witnessed John's condition but no one dared to say anything, everyone was anxious, John was in horrible form, but he still suggested that they keep going since no one knows when another assault would befall them; everybody was dubious, but they all agreed to anything John said at this point in time. consequently, they all left camp and began walking their route. Back at the camp, Bart was badly wounded but nevertheless surviving. He struggled to stand but collapsed every time. He looked around and realized that all of his crew members had died. He realized he was the only person who had survived. As he began to move, he discovered that his leg was covered in blood. He soon noticed that his hand was bleeding. It was tough to move because of this.

When John and Aiden's group got close to the gas station, they spotted a road block.

"What exactly is this?" Aiden stated......

"They look infected!" Kyle said "What are they up to?" "They're hiding something." Ruthven responded.

They approached the infected group and began firing at them; all of the infected killed, and they observed a guy passed out in a car, locking himself inside to protect himself from the infected.

John attempted to shatter the car window, but this just drew more infected people in. They tried to eliminate the infected persons; however, they were constantly surrounded. "There's no meaning, see, we're running out on fire power, HIDE UNDER THE CARS," John said. They decided to hide beneath the cars to avoid attracting further infected. They all huddled beneath the car, undetected by the infected. When one of the infected observed Mike's injured legs, he attempted to seize him. The survivor shot the infected within the car and handed Mike his hand. "Are you all right?" said by the survivor in the car...."I'm totally fine." Mike responded....

"Are you okay, Mike?" Ruthven inquired.

John expressed gratitude to the survivor for saving Mike. "Everything is OK. What is your name? Are you a virus-infected murderous gang?" the survivor stated. "Something along those lines, but what were you doing here by yourself?" Ruthven inquired....

"I wasn't the only one. I had a similar group as you. My family was around, but they perished." Survivor responded.......

"I'm sorry," John said......

"Is this your son?" Survivor inquired...

"Yes," John said.

"I had too. Kim was his name."

"We were hiding from the infected when an infected snatched my son's leg and bit him. It was too late for me to save him." Lo and behold a shot was fired, alerting everyone. They had been followed by a group of survivors....

"What the- "We can't get any rest," Kyle stated... "Aiden! Aiden! Where are you? You rat, you". John locked his gaze on Aiden. "What?" Aiden stated. "Why is the entire world after you?" John stated... "Come on Aiden, you can't win because we outnumber you." Aiden stared at John and told him he needs to go. John disagreed and urged him to remain hidden, but Aiden had other plans, therefore he strolled out and tried to say, "Oh man, this guy! ..."

"There you have it! My dear Aiden!" a survivor stated "What do you want?" Aiden inquired. Survivor said, "You know what I want."...

"What!" ....

"Revenge, you killed my crew and my brother." Survivor yelled....

"I'm sorry, who?" Aiden asked....

"My brother." Survivor said....

"I've never met your goddamn brother." Aiden responded. "BART!" Aiden knew who he was referring to, "James?" Aiden stated.

"You remember me." James said "I was going to give you another chance, but after what you've done to me, US! "I want you to die." James said

When John spotted a vehicle leaking gas, he pointed it towards Kyle. He saw the car and was ready to shoot. Ruthven and Aiden's team were instructed by John to keep focused and ready for action. Aiden's team reloaded their rifles and prepared to shoot.

James was still conversing with Aiden. "Aiden, you were a nice guy, and I'm sorry it had to come to this." James said

Barry pointed the gun at Aiden, and the shot was fired. The car exploded, injuring James and his team. John took advantage of the situation and fired. Aiden drew out his gun and pointed it towards James' head. When James turned back, he saw his whole crew dead. "How about the turn tables?" James said as Aiden replied, "Goodbye, James."

Aiden shot him and moved on. When they arrived, they saw the survivor who had rescued Mike had been shot by James's crew member. They couldn't do anything and kept moving. "Is this the end?" Aiden inquired. "This is it," John said. They noticed a large gate packed with survivors. They kept their eyes vigilant whatsoever costs. John, Aiden, Kyle, and Ruthven edged closer to the gate. Other survivors stayed.... "What brings you here?" says the survivor

"I'd want to meet Sierra." John stated...

"What is your name?" a survivor stated..."My name is John. It's important." John stated…

"We decide if it's important or not," the survivor stated.

The door was opened with a creaking sound, and the very first thing they witnessed was Sierra standing directly in front of them. "You returned. Why?" Sierra said......

"We don't have to go to war with them." John stated. "Uh, you don't understand anything, do you?" Sierra said.......

"The boss, usually goes by Adrien." John responded…

"I have someone who could help us." John stated.

Sierra looked perplexed and said, "What? Who?" Should we come in first?" John responded with a gentle smile. Sierra took John and peered around at the other survivors. They entered the Armory tent, where John told them all they needed to know about Aiden and how they could prevent this fight. "So, he had a brother, and you think he'll let us all go if we show him his brother?" Sierra inquired, perplexed. "What are you seeking to say?"....

"We go in and try to speak with him." John responded. "What are you talking about?" Sierra said "Do you think they'll simply let us talk?"....

"So, what are we going to do now?" John inquired.
"We need to slip in." Sierra responded...
"It would be more difficult this way." John stated...
"So, why don't you go ahead and give it a shot? He'll shoot you without even listening to you, believe me, I know what he's like. He's changed, he might not be his best buddy's brother or whatever" Sierra said…
"We have backups, and we might be able to reach him." Sierra said......

"All right, fine." John inquired. "What's the plan?" "Gather around, I'll explain." Sierra said everyone congregated in the Armory area, including Aiden's and Sierra's crews. Sierra began by explaining the strategy to everyone. The strategy proved impractical. There were several questions. The plan was set to go into effect at midnight tomorrow. While others were perplexed, debating, and constantly asking questions, John stood and listened. Sierra adjourned the meeting and exited the place. She was later joined by John, who counseled her to reconsider her approach. She had already made up her mind and refused to change her decision, claiming that it would work.

John gradually stepped away from the conversation, and as he met Aiden a few feet ahead, Aiden said, "John, we need to talk." John saw it coming since he assumed he came to discuss Sierra's proposal, but he was instantly rebutted. Aiden invited John to accompany him outdoors, to which John replied, "Why, what's the matter?"

"We need to gather some supplies because Mike is sick." Aiden expressed his anguish as he gazed at John. "WHAT HAPPENED?" John was flabbergasted.

Aiden urged John to follow him immediately to obtain supplies since they wouldn't have much time and Mike's life may be in jeopardy. John didn't knew anything, but he consented and went out with Aiden without reluctance. They both started heading out when they watched Sierra rushing towards the medical tent. John hurriedly hailed her and said, "What happened?" Sierra was silent for a moment before softly telling John, "You should go, it's not the right time." Sierra went instantly. "Can somebody just tell what the hell is going on?" shouted John. Aiden soon approached him, saying, "We don't know, but please come for Mike's sake."

Kyle ran into Sierra and asked her what was going on and why John was suddenly yelling. Sierra first tried ignoring Kyle, but as soon as Ruthven and Anna joined Kyle, she blurted, "Mike, He got bitte-bitten."
"What! We should tell John!" Anna spoke out right away........

"No, we can't because it's too late to help him." Sierra spoke rapidly and regretfully. "We lack the vaccination."......

"Are you insane, John is the father he deserves to know," Kyle said.

"Listen, I can't guarantee Mike's survival, but it might be feasible to do something about it, which is why I sent them to acquire the medication." Sierra exclaimed...

"You understand, once John comes, the first thing you'd tell him is about Mike's bite mark?" Ruthven replied as she moved away from the discussion. Kyle was spacing out since everything was happening so rapidly. He realized everything has been buggered up and didn't know what's what, so he went to his tent to clear his head. Anna, on the other hand, stood near the medication tent, trying to catch a glimpse of Mike. She was genuinely frightened about him.

SEVEN

The Execution

John and Aiden performed an errand. They observed all the abandoned places, but none of them had infected. Aiden stared at John, perplexed. Aiden's ideas were matched by John......

"It's rare for places like these to be infected-free." John inquired "Where is the medical store?"...

"These clubs and medical supply businesses should be swarming with infected people." Aiden expressed his bewilderment......

"You believe someone must have cleared them." As he retrieved his gun from his gun belt, John remarked...
"I believe so. Should we check those?" Aiden responded
"How much time do we have? We critically want medications" John said

Aiden mentioned that they had ample time to search around the pharmaceutical shop, so they did just that. They both walked inside and sought for the necessary medication. John endeavored to find the appropriate supply but failed; Aiden, on the other hand, was also unable to locate the required supply; John reached the conclusion that they should investigate other locations that had the potential to obtain the appropriate medication for Mike.

Aiden suggested seeing another medical shop nearby the abandoned streets; John nodded without hesitation, and they both moved. As they walked out, they stumbled upon an infected nest that was obstructing their path. This was Aiden's first encounter with an infected nest. He was perplexed and questioned John what was it and how they were supposed to traverse the street. Aiden was swiftly advised by John to destroy the nest and keep moving.

"All right, then let's do it." Aiden stated as he pulled a large machete from his backpack. He was about to attack when John stopped him and said, "Don't-

Aiden came to a standstill, baffled, and questioned John, "For what?"....

"You can't just swing a machete at it." These infected are still alive, and if we attack them, more infected will spring up and kill us." John responded

"There are just five infected people." We can destroy them." Aiden stated as he checked the infected nest...
"It usually appears that there aren't many, but the big thing is what's underneath it and, there could be hundreds or more, so if we attack even one of them, they'll rouse the rest up and surround us in no time," John explained......

"That's why we found no infected." Aiden stated

"How, exactly, should we clean the nest? "...
"We must burn it." John stated "Do you have something that can set fire to it?"

John spotted a lighter protruding from an infected. He alerted Aiden regarding it and silently tried to seize it. The infected did not react upon first, but when John used the lighter, the infected awoke, which startled both John and Aiden......

"Light it up quickly." Aiden spoke...

"I'm trying! Hang on a minute!"

The infected were emerging from every direction, even the ground. Although John and Aiden were fearful, John was able to ignite the nest before it was too late. The nest smoldered. John and Aiden removed several infected that had already escaped from the nest. The path was finally cleared; thus, they were able to reach the next medical store across.

John rushed in and was instantly attacked by infected, although he was ready to take care of it, whilst Aiden was successful in retrieving the needed medicine for Mike. He and John immediately dashed out of the store and headed to Sierra's camp. Anna visited Ruthven back at camp. She approached him and reported him that Mike had turned and was being held in a secure cell. "What!" Ruthven responded, his jaw dropping...

Anna asked Ruthven to examine on his own. Kyle noticed them and opted to join them. They all witnessed the infected cell, there were several infected behind the cells, and Mike wasn't the only person held there. Sierra was already standing outside Mike's cell as Anna approached it and saw Mike turning into such an infected. She became distraught and couldn't control herself and began weeping. Ruthven approached Sierra and spoke about Mike. "We knew he was bitten when he suddenly became limp, We discovered a bite mark on his leg." Sierra stated,"

Ruthven observed his bite mark and kept his head low; Sierra, on the other end, watched Anna becoming tearful and approached her, saying, "Don't worry, we won't let him suffer."....

"Wait!! WHAT? Are you going to shoot him?" Kyle inquired as he ran between Sierra and Anna's conversation.

"How is that a shitty thing?" Sierra stated as she stared Ruthven in the sight. "So, you're basically going to kill him and not even tell his father?" Kyle was enraged... "We don't have a choice; we have to." Sierra said. "Do you realize how insane you sound?" Kyle said. "No, there is always a choice," Anna whispered...

"Look, I admire your efforts, but don't tell John about them until we carry out our plan." Sierra said as she stormed out of the room, and Kyle confronted Ruthven, saying, "We are making ridiculous sacrifices for those people, people like Sierra, you seriously believe John would indeed be happy seeing us hiding the news of Mike off him purely because a person named Sierra instructed us too, RUTHVEN TELL ME!!"

Anna paused them and said, "Whatever happens, this is important for John to know," and also that "Mike would've have wished the same to see his father for the last time, because none of us knows who's going to survive or die out there in this ridiculous mission.". "She's right, Ruthven." Kyle stated as he left the tent. Anna also left after a few seconds. Ruthven looked at Mike, said his final goodbyes, and walked out of the tent, with dejected expression on his face. Sierra passed Ruthven on her way and approached him. "Don't get distracted, Ruthven; we have a mission." Sierra said...

"I'd known him for a long time. It's upsetting to watch our loved ones suffering from this infection." Ruthven stated "I was surprised when John told me that he cared about Anna despite the fact that he hadn't known her for long, however he appeared to love her like his own daughter."......

"I apologize. I'll give you a moment. Meet me after that". Sierra said....

"I was with John and Mike when the apocalypse began, you see, we were able to escape together, we exited the city. That was my final scenario with my family." Ruthven stated......

"I apologize-......

"Don't be, just tell John about Mike. He should be aware of this." Ruthven stated...

"Alright, he should be here by now. You should see him." Sierra said as she left while Ruthven walked past the tents towards the gate. He waited for John to return, and also to his amazement, Kyle was also waiting there, seeing Ruthven and asking, "What are you doing here?" Ruthven remained silent for a few seconds before saying, "I am waiting for John." Kyle gave him a frown and inquired if he was there to confront John about Mike.......

"I surely will." Ruthven replied softly.

Kyle waited for John beside Ruthven. They noticed two survivors and mistook them for John and Aiden.

"Something doesn't seem right." Kyle expressed his curiosity about the two people approaching them. Ruthven asked one of the survivors to identify the two survivors while they were guarding the gate...

"Who are they?" Ruthven inquired.

The two survivors were coming closer to the gate when they yelled, "WAIT! Do not fire-...

"Who are you?!" The guards at the gate questioned the two survivors and pointed a gun at them...
"WE DO NOT WANT ANY PROBLEMS-...

"Please contact Sierra." one of the security guards stated.
"What's going on?" Sierra stated on the other end of the radio.

Sierra was alerted about the Survivors outside the gate, so she ordered them to take them inside the interrogation room. They took in the two living survivors.

The Undead Bonds

The survivors were injured and appeared to have barely survived. Sierra entered the tent. She observed that they had some paperwork on them, but they weren't armed......

"What is your name?" Sierra inquired, she gaze dead in their eyes.......

"My name is Jack, and his name is Kim."...
"What are you doing here?" Sierra inquired...

"We were on a mission when we were attacked by infected people." We barely made it. Jack remained silent while Kim spoke.

Sierra said, "Where were you going?"...

"Through the valley, just ahead of this camp." Kim replied

Sierra tried to ask them more questions, but both Kim and Jack refused to give her anything about their plan, Sierra became furious and ordered her crew to restrain them until the mission was completed successfully. Sierra had left the tent and was walking back to her tent when she realized the gate was opened and she couldn't find Ruthven or Kyle. She realized what had resulted and dashed to the infected room, where John was already grieving in front of his son....

"Hey, I'm so sorry for-

John sprang to his feet and dashed over to Sierra. In rage, he pulled out the gun and pointed it at her, intending to kill her. "You deserve to die." As he wept, John stated....

"Wait a minute, listen to me." Sierra said....

"What's the point? You were not going to tell me anything about him. I'm grateful to Ruthven and Kyle for telling me about him. You let him turn." John stated "It was always your fault!"....

"Wait, listen, I tried to save him. Even our medical team tried, but we were incapable to do well." Sierra expressed her fear....

"You couldn't do a basic job and were planning to kill the boss of a gang that runs a city with tens of thousands of people. Give me one good reason why I shouldn't kill you ". John stated....

"You cannot." Sierra said....

"I can. I am stronger than you and your crew!". John stated......

"Look around you at all the cells and infected people. Your son died as a result of an infection. Because of that, I lost my family. They were all close to me. How do you think I felt in front of my mother, father, and two brothers? ". Sierra said

Everyone looked at the cells that were filled with infected inside, John was shocked so were Ruthven and Kyle. "John, I am sorry for your loss." Sierra said as she stepped out of the tent slowly. Once John glanced around, he noticed that everyone was infected. They were all named according to who they were and how they turned up. "Can you please leave me alone for a second? I'd like to be alone, but Anna, please stay with me ". John stated....

"Sure." Ruthven and Kyle stated as they exited the tent. The grief-stricken John refused to leave his dead Son's side Time swiftly passed, and the moment arrived when the plan was finally put into action. Everyone had come except John, who was still taking his time in the armory area. He came after a few minutes and was straightaway questioned by Sierra whether he was ready and prepared for the plan. John raised his head and replied, "Yes."

The plan was supposed to be carried out at midnight, but it was decided that since they have Aiden's aid, they will carry it out right immediately. Sierra directed her crew, as well as John and Aiden's crews, to go ahead and begin their section first. John and Aiden both stepped in via a massive gate and found the entire place rotting. A few steps ahead, they observed a fully functional casino, which appeared exactly like any other, with a large number of people moving in and out. John and Aiden began to make their way towards Adrien's casino. Sierra returned to the tent and began prepping the rest of the crew. She pulled out a map of the city and began presenting it to everyone else........

"You all know what to do, but let's go through it again. John and Aiden plan to gamble inside the casino. There will be a guy called Alex. He is one of Adrien's most loyal bodyguards. In an emergency, only he has access to him. We must remove him first so that no one may contact him about the next attack." Sierra said...

"How are we going to upset him again?" Kyle inquired...

"Leave that to John and Aiden." Sierra said "He'll send us a signal when they upset him. That is where we will collapse the casino."

A survivor stopped John and Aiden from passing through the gate. He was the casino's security guard. "What is your name?" What brings you here? "What's the code?"

"My name is Caleb, and Won is my companion. We are from the valley's 78th section." John said....

"THE CODE-

John shot the security guard in the head and continued. As they passed, one of the casino employees approached them and said, "How are you doing, fellas? We have a unique contest where you may win firearms and bullets. The winner receives the unique "famous gun."......
"What kind of gun?" Aiden inquired given that he was seeking to acquire the gun....

"We can't reveal it until you join in the contest," the casino employee explained....

"Uh, we're OK." While glancing at Aiden, John stated. "Makes you so sure? You appear to be a professional shooter" the casino employee stated...

"Nah, I'm just here to play a little poker." John responded.

As John turned to face Aiden, the employee's smile began to fade as John told him that they should leave. John went searching for Alex. He spotted a man in armor, a vest, and surrounded by bodyguards. He instantly told Aiden to check. Aiden was first skeptical, but when he said that he may be Alex, they both began heading towards him. They approached him to see what was going on.

When they arrived, they struck eye contact with the employee who had earlier invited them to join in the event. "So, you guys finally showed up," the employee said.

Because of him, John became agitated and muttered, "What's wrong with him, shit?"

Aiden inquired about the man wearing armor and surrounded by security.

"Oh, he's the owner of this casino; he's only here today because of the event; normally, it's difficult to see him." employee stated. John continued his inquiry by inquiring about Alex. "Alex?" said the employee, his voice got relatively low and gravelly. "How do you know him?"

When John watched the employee's smile slip away again, he realized something was amiss if they repeated inquiring about Alex to everyone, so he answered, "Oh, a guy told- never mind, when does the contest starts?"

He sat beside Aiden after checking at all the seats that were positioned right in front of a little stage. Suddenly, he noticed the employee mumbling something to that large man who had all the bodyguards surrounding him, and that gentleman stared at John for a split second before looking away and whispering something back to the employee......

"On the row, gentleman! Hey! -

"John, it's your turn, go forward," Aiden urged, tapping on John's shoulder.

The employee approached the organizer on stage who had just summoned John on stage and stated something to him discreetly and slowly; John became bewildered and suspicious but still proceeded to the stage. The organizer directed him to sit on one of the chairs offered on stage, and when he did, they chained him to the chair. "Hey!!" What the hell are you doing?!?" shouted John

Suddenly, the organizer emerged and informed him that this was all part of the competition. Aiden wished to help John but was unable to do so. When John was shackled to the chair, he was dragged onto the stage and swung from an infected chain around his neck. "What the hell is this?" John stated

The organizer took the stage and began outlining what was about to happen in this contest in a sarcastic and thrilling style. John wasn't really looking good and asked them repeatedly what they were planning to do with him. The organizer announced that the participant would have two minutes to free themselves from the infected.

What?

The organizer went on to say that if that person did not comply, the infected would be unleashed and the participant would be killed by the infected. The organizer turned and went away. John was startled and immediately attempted to untie himself. Sierra was still in the camp, waiting for the signal. "What's taking them so long?" Kyle inquired as he stood outside the tent with Ruthven, who was fully prepared with the crew and weaponry.......

"ONE MINUTE LEFT"

Aiden was watching him struggle to untie himself, everybody else were watching and seeking amusement, however for John it was a race for his life, he quickly attempted to break free but discovered that the entire stage is covered with explosives underneath it, he also realized that if he tried to pull the ropes too hard, he would eventually set up the bombs himself and would die, he knew he was sat on a death trap. He saw that he was the only one on stage, which meant that everything regarding the infected and the bombs was already planned. ***"RELEASE THE INFECTED"***

When John glanced up, he saw the infected coming towards him. Aiden noticed the infected racing and pulled out his rifle to kill the infected. Everyone was stunned as he shot the infected in the head. "Who shot????" Alex said

"There he is, our man!" Aiden said as Alex spotted Aiden and approached him angrily. "How did you get a weapon inside the property?" Alex inquired. "

It's none of your business-

He aimed his gun towards Alex and told him to keep silent. Alex smiled and reached for his revolver, but he was cut short by John......

"You got away?" Alex was taken aback and stated. "I got away within few seconds. This was planned. Everything was a ruse." John stated. Even Aiden was taken aback since he had no idea John was pretending to be trapped there and that this had been part of John's plan all along. John had numerous thoughts racing through his mind; he had no idea about the explosives beneath him; he understood he was alive by a miracle because if he had acted more like he was struggling, he may have died. "You scumbags!" Alex said "What were you hoping to achieve here?"....

"We already have." Aiden responded as Sierra and her team suddenly crashed the casino, and the mission was officially begun. Everyone in the casino was unarmed except Alex's bodyguards. Without hesitation, John shot Alex and a battle ensued; within seconds, Sierra's crew was able to knock down Alex's bodyguards. Other people in the casino began to fight with their bare hands, but they were shortly shot by Aiden and John.

The survivors were scattered throughout the casino. One of them realized Alex had a pistol on his body. He grabbed the gun fast and shot one of the Sierra's crew men. After that, he was repeatedly shot....

"We lost one," Sierra said. "We have to keep moving." They sped past the casino and arrived to an abandoned police station.

They gazed ahead and noticed a massive edifice at the end. "That's where we have to go," Sierra added. "All well, then." John stated. The door was barred with chains and a large lock. They smashed it and broke in. The area was infested with infected. It appeared that no one had been there for years.

The crew moved rapidly into position and killed the infected. "The path is clear; let's go." Kyle said. They proceeded down the corridor and saw the door was barred from the outside.......

"We have to find a different way." John stated. They were trying to figure out how to escape from the other side when they were interrupted by a loud bang. They peered along the deserted corridor. Nobody was around. The big bang was heard yet again. The bang was becoming increasingly deafening. "I believe someone is approaching." Anna stated. Everyone was staring down the corridor. With each stride, the bang became louder. Aiden could see what was approaching and hurriedly ordered everyone to leave.

Everyone was so puzzled that they kept asking them what was going on, to which Aiden responded, "It's a level four infected."....

"They now have levels!!" Sierra expressed her amazement but remained anxious.

As the infected approached, everyone heeded Aiden's command and began running, except for John and Ruthven, who were prepared to fight him. "What are you up to?" Aiden was perplexed....

"We have no choice except to kill him." Ruthven stated confidentially...."We can't kill him!" Aiden stated. While walking, the infected began shattering the ceiling and doors. In front of everyone, he entered the main hallway. "What the hell is that?" Ruthven expressed his fear.

Because of his bulk, the infected could hardly move along the corridor. He spotted the crew and dashed towards them. He was demolishing the entire corridor, giving John and Sierra's team time to flee, but because of this damage, more infected were drawn to them as well. Everyone dashed for the stairs since that was the only way around.......

"Climb to the roof." Sierra gave the order as she headed up the stairs. They dashed up the stairwell. Because the infected was unable to climb, he became enraged and began damaging the staircase.

The majority of the Sierra's crew men perished, while the others narrowly made it to the top....

"I guess he won't be able to come here." With a sigh of relief, John replied

They remained on the roof. "I need to catch my breath." Ruthven stated

"Guys!"....

"What is it, Kyle?" In a sour attitude, John remarked, "I suppose he's here." Kyle spoke in a slow tone. When John looked at the shattered stairs, he noticed that the infected had jump through the walls. He seized the survivors who were close to the collapsed staircases. "How did he manage to get up here?" Sierra inquired, Perplexed

They concluded that killing the infected was the only way to survive, so they executed just that. "Everyone, hold him with all your force!!" Sierra commanded

They all began shooting the infected but were surprised to find the infected still standing without being injured. Sierra said, "Does this bullet even harm him?" They continued to fire, but the infected remained unharmed.

The shots did not appear to have any effect on the infected.......

"We need to come up with something different." With a puzzled expression on his face, John remarked.

Aiden, on the other hand, had a grand idea, so he called John and asked, "John, do you still have the lighter?" "Yeah, what about it?" John responded right away.

Aiden instantly called Kyle, described his proposal to Kyle, and both agreed without hesitation. "Aiden, whatever you plan to do, do it quickly." John stated. "John, have the Molotov cocktail fired up and ready to throw when I say." Aiden stated as he took his position. Aiden emerged from the cover and yelled, "Everyone, stop firing and make no noise!"

Nobody listened to him at first, but as John shouted after him, everyone turned to look at him, and not a single bullet went through the gun after that. Everyone had come to a standstill. They took a peek at the infected. He was still standing there, not attempting to attack them. Aiden grabbed a grenade and tossed it to the infected side. "What are you doing?" John said quietly.......

"The infected levels three and four are powerful, but they can't see anything. They are only drawn by sound." Aiden stated. "We can't just run or walk away; he'll hear us.".....

"All right, so what's the plan?" Sierra said as Aiden directed everyone to this side and began detailing his strategy, instructing everyone to remain in their current positions. Aiden stood up and grabbed a grenade. He approached one of the towers, connected a time grenade, and tossed another at the other. He hurled the final grenade near the wrecked chopper.

When the infected arrived at the helicopter, the timed grenade detonated, causing the towers to collapse directly on him and the chopper. The helicopter began to leak. Aiden instructed John to light the Molotov cocktail.

The Molotov cocktail was thrown correctly and exploded, taking the chopper and the infected with it......

"We should get going. I have a bad feeling ". Sierra said as The crew began to move slowly, they got close to the damaged staircase, but they were wrecked and overrun. "We can't pass through here," Aiden said. "We have to find a different way." John took a step to the edge of the roof. Aiden turned to face him. He approached him, and they both noticed a shattered tower attached to the top of a supermarket.... "Do you believe we can cross through here?" Aiden inquired, peering through the damaged tower, which appeared difficult and perilous to walk through. "I believe so, although it appears strange." John stated.

"How come?" Aiden inquired, perplexed....

"I believe someone has already been through here." John stated......

Sierra heard John from afar and instantly joined them in disbelief, exclaiming, "What! "Do you think so?"

"Yes, have a look, all the roofs are connected by a bridge that is either a broken tower or planks that joins every single top," John explained as he pointed out all the rooftops. "It had to be Adrien." Sierra said. "Or it's possible that someone like us snuck in." John stepped in.....

"You mean there are more survivors?" Sierra responded with a solemn expression...."There is a possibility." John stated "We must continue. Try to keep your eyes open at all times." Sierra turned to her crew, and they began to move. John began to move after looking towards Ruthven and Kyle.

They began to cross. The tower was still standing, but it was difficult to use as a bridge for a large crew..."Everyone, watch your steps." Sierra gave the order after reaching the other side. Anna was the final one to cross.

John extended his hand to her and they stretched towards the other roof. "Do we just keep doing this till we get to the end?" Sierra said. according John, they have no option but to follow these bridges because they will be the fastest and mostly infected-free. They began to make their way towards the second bridge. The bridge was still intact, which was surprising given how badly damaged it had been...

"Are you sure we can cross?" Sierra said...

"We don't have any other choice," John said. The crew began strolling across the bridge. It was dilapidated, yet it could carry a few passengers at a time. Sierra and Anna were the first to make the crossing. Aiden was asked to cross next by John. He began crossing the bridge, but it began to creak. Aiden successfully crossed the bridge, but it was severely damaged. Sierra was warned by John that they wouldn't be able to cross the bridge because it would collapse on them. "So, how are you going to cross?" Sierra inquired....

"We'll figure something out." John stated "But, you should move."

The only people that were able to cross the bridge were Sierra, Anna, and Aiden. The others were with John, attempting to figure out another approach...

"You should go; I will catch up." John stated...

"My crew is with you; get over here quickly." Sierra said.

John stared at Sierra and promptly began to seek for another route.

He instructed Ruthven and Kyle to seek for the greatest feasible approach in other ways. They split up. Ruthven discovered a broken floor on the roof a few steps ahead. He quickly called Kyle and told him to pass through here.

Kyle proposed that only they should go at first, which Ruthven agreed to, and they stepped through......

"You guys, stay right here." Ruthven said "We'll be back."......

"I'll come with you," one of Sierra's crew members responded. "I believe I could be of use to you."

Ruthven and Kyle were unconcerned and plunged in with the survivor, and they all got in. It was a shattered supermarket......

"This seems to be a mess." Ruthven stated as he checked the entire shop...."What happened here?" Kyle stated, "Did the infected perpetrate this?"

The store was full with skeletons and was rather old. Since the virus spread, it appeared that no one had gone inside. "So, this is what seven years of infection looks like." Ruthven stated as Kyle approached one of the skeletons and noticed a note in its hand. The note mentioned a family who had been abandoned by the military.

The note said,

Walt is my name. I had a family. Michael was the name of my son. When the infection began, he was 13 years old. I was at home, talking to my kid about his future plans. He aspired to be a professional athlete. He earned a gold medal in a school event, and then the news channel began reporting about an infection that was fast spreading among humans.

They advised us not to leave our house and to remain where we were. They advised us to leave the city before dawn, as the infection was spreading so quickly that we would be stranded at our house for who knows how long. We attempted to escape, but the infection spread quickly, and the roads were clogged with either people like us trying to escape the city or infected trying to attack us.

We made it through and onto the freeway, but that wasn't the end of it. It was jammed. There were many others trying to escape the infection. We stepped out of the car and began walking as quickly as we could to keep ourselves safe, but we were not the luckiest.

One of the infected attacked us. We managed to drive the infected away and leave. My son was really exhausted. He tried to run, but he wasn't feeling good. Suddenly, the military arrived to save us. They noticed Michael and instantly left. They pulled a pistol at him.

Back then, he was bitten by an infection. He had no idea he had been infected. He tried to shout aloud my name. He was in anguish and pleading with me to save him, but the military killed him right in front of me due to his infection.

His mother died when he was four, leaving just me to care for him. This virus devastated it, and it is currently destroying everything mankind has accomplished.

"What happens next?" Ruthven inquired....

"I'm not sure, it was torn down after that." Kyle responded.......

"All right, let's leave; we can't afford to waste any more time." Ruthven stated, he and the survivor began to walk, but Kyle remained still. Ruthven returned his look and approached him, inquiring as to what had happened. Kyle turned to face him and said, "This story reminded me of Mike." Ruthven tapped him on the shoulder. Even he became upset and responded, "I know."

Kyle's mood suddenly altered and he became perplexed as he peered behind Ruthven and noticed a type of virus hooked to a table, which moved from time to time. They were awake and moving about on their own. When the survivor stated that he was aware of the infection, Kyle and Ruthven immediately asked as to what it was.......

"These infections are like plants; they move on their own but only if the infected, or infected host, is around." says the survivor. The virus approached them, and it appeared that they were drawn to humans. The survivor saw this and stated that this infection need two things in order to move on its own....

"What are they?" Kyle inquired....

"First, they require the infected who have spread these viruses, and second, they require a group of survivors; even three individuals are sufficient to get them rolling on their own." says the survivor....

"Do you believe he's here?" Kyle said...

"He should be here." Survivor responded "These infections attract a wide range of people."...

They soon realized something, "That means-

Three of them dashed towards the survivors, making it to the rooftops......

"Where is everyone?" Ruthven stated "Check the other roofs," the survivor replied, running around looking for everyone. Kyle stepped onto the plank. It was feeble, but it got Kyle to the other side. He looked for Sierra on the other roofs. Ruthven and the survivor continued on their pathway. They began looking for John and Sierra's crew. Ruthven searched all the adjacent roofs and streets visible from that vantage point, noticing the survivor staring at something and thinking he could have discovered any of the other survivors. He promptly inquired as to what he was looking at, and the survivor pointed to the infection. He revealed to Ruthven that the infection was travelling on its own and that the host was likely nearby. "Look closely, Ruthven." He stated....

"So that means," Ruthven continued, realizing the source of the infected movement.

We should get moving." Survivor stated...

"Wait-..."Who are you? How did you find out about the level five infection?" Ruthven enquired....

"My name is Nate."....

"How about the infection?" How do you know?" Ruthven enquired.

Kyle shouted from the opposite side. He yelled Ruthven's name. Ruthven gazed at him. Kyle was tense. He phoned Ruthven yet again. "What's the problem?" He inquired as he stood beside Nate. Kyle was out of breath. "LEVEL FIVE!" he yelled.

Nate mentioned that one of them is also around. He suggested Ruthven to help Kyle with the infected and assured him that he could manage the infected over here. "Don't die," Ruthven muttered, looking at him...

"Good luck in there." Ruthven stated

Nate returned his smile and dallied. Ruthven ran over to Kyle. He attempted to take a step on the plank, but as he was about to take another, the plank snapped, causing him to fall through the ceiling. After collapsing, he fought to get back up. Kyle dashed to the edge, where he spotted Ruthven dangling. He reached out his hand to him. "Come on, just grab it." Kyle said. Ruthven successfully climbed up by grasping his hand. He chased him down.

"Which way are we going?" Ruthven inquired.

Kyle stayed silent as he ran forward, and they both leaped onto the other roof. They were crossing via the bridges. Kyle abruptly halted. They were on the roof of a large structure that had been infected. It was screwed up. The infection was spreading quicker than ever before. "Where are the others?" Ruthven enquired...

"Follow me inside." Kyle answered....

"We're going to die in there." Ruthven stated "Are you sure there are people in there?"....

"I overheard Sierra." Kyle responded. "We must save her."......

"Do you know how to go in?" Ruthven inquired.

Kyle took a glance at the door. It was infected to the point that they couldn't get in. Ruthven looked at the door and told Kyle that they couldn't walk in. Kyle snatched a Molotov cocktail from his rucksack and hurled it towards the infected. They began to burn, creating a path through the steps....

"Do you have a machete or something sharp?" Kyle inquired.

Ruthven gave him with a machete. Kyle got a cloth from his bag and began wrapping it around the machete. He then set fire to the cloth and began going towards the infection. He swiftly pierced the infection.

The Undead Bonds

Ruthven followed him all the way. "How deep does this go?" Ruthven inquired.

Kyle said, "Just up ahead." They were able to break through all of the infection. The infection was spreading, making it difficult for them to continue. They eventually made it through and arrived in an empty hallway. "It's completely empty." Kyle said "They've left."

For a few seconds, there was silence. Ruthven continued to search. Then he was startled by a startling sound in the doorway. He looked at Kyle, and they both began to go toward the doorway. Nothing was there as they peered through the door. Kyle advised Ruthven to keep his guard up at all times. They moved slowly towards the rear. The fire suddenly went out, and the room became much darker than before, with not a single sound. Ruthven told Kyle to relight the machete. He gave Kyle the lighter to ignite, but it didn't take long for the infected to find their way to the building. Kyle and Ruthven had no idea the infected had arrived. Kyle eventually lighted the machete and urged Ruthven to follow him to the entrance through which they came. Ruthven ran back to the door, only to find himself surrounded by infected. The number of infected people was growing. Kyle and Ruthven were constantly killing them, but they were still unable to pass through the entrance. "We are outnumbered by the infected." Kyle said

He attempted to burn them with his Molotov, but the infected were not dying and were not diminishing in number. The infected continued to enter. Ruthven kept attempting to clear their way so they could leave the location they came from, but there were so many of them that no matter how hard they tried, it wasn't enough to kill them all.

Ruthven had lost all hope as a result of this movement. "I suppose this is it." Ruthven lamented. Kyle continued to shoot the infected.......

"Did you not hear me? STOP! It's over for us!" Ruthven stated as he grabbed Kyle's arm and told him to stop firing. Kyle refused and continued to blast through the infected.......

"What's the matter, Kyle?" Ruthven inquired...
"We can't afford to lose." Kyle said...

"But we've already lost." Ruthven stated…

"We just cannot afford to lose." Kyle said...

"But it's already finished." Ruthven stated...
"John would not have liked this." I'm sure he would have done the same if he were here. He'd keep killing them even if the odds were stacked against him. He would not have surrendered that easily. Even Mike placed our life ahead of his own."

Ruthven whispered gently, "Kyle-"...

"We've lost a lot of people already, and I can't lose you or myself." Kyle responded.

"We must do it-...

"For Mike."

Ruthven began to shoot and began killing a large number of infected with everything he could get his hands on. It was a heated battleground. The infected continued to enter. Ruthven had a lot of ammunition to keep the infected away....

"I'm almost out," Ruthven remarked....

"Just keep going," Kyle said. "I'm almost out too."

They were continuously shooting and killing infected people. Ruthven ran out of ammunition and was attacked by an infected. He shoved him away swiftly, but more infected followed.

Kyle killed one of the infected that was attacking Ruthven. He attempted to shoot the other infected, but he ran out of ammunition. All of the infected jumped on them. They kicked a few infected, but there were a lot more of them storming onto them.......

"Give me a hand, Kyle," Ruthven urged....

"I can hardly move; I don't know how I'm still alive." Kyle responded.

Suddenly, the floor began to shake, forcing the infected off and causing them to collapse. The floor began to crack. Ruthven stumbled out and collapsed. "Ruthven, are you okay?" Kyle inquired. He jumped down as Ruthven told him, since it was the only way, they might survive.

Ruthven took out sprinting as soon as Kyle jumped. Kyle followed him, and they both began racing towards the door in order to escape. Ruthven unexpectedly came to a stop as they approached the door. Kyle noticed him and grabbed his hand, pulling him close to the entrance, but Ruthven stopped him....

"KYLE, NO." Ruthven said "It's all over."

Kyle was perplexed and mumbled, "What? What do you mean? Let's go!"....

"I- can't," Ruthven murmured, a pained expression on his face........

"What the heck are you talking about-?

Ruthven rolled up his sleeves and showed Kyle a bite mark; Kyle struggled to accept it, but he persisted in urging him to get out of here since there could be a vaccination. Ruthven continued imploring Kyle that he needed to go save his own life, but Kyle insisted on leaving with him.

"KYLE!! You have people to save, and they need your help!! GO TO THEM, you still have JOHN, ANNA, they need you more than I do, GOOO!!!!"

The infected eventually came up to them and began pouring on them, Ruthven grabbed Kyle and shoved him out the door, throwing his rucksack at him for some more supplies and closing the door on his face. Kyle pounded on the door, yelling, "RUTHVEN!!"

Ruthven had somehow shut the door from the other side, Sierra and Anna were able to reach Kyle after hearing his voice from afar. "Kyle! What happened? Are you alright?" Sierra inquired. Kyle came to a halt and held a gun at Sierra's head, stating while sobbing. "It's completely your fault! People are dying as a result of your plan! It's all your fault!"

Anna stood there, quiet, but she could hear the agony in Kyle's voice; she became melancholy but managed to keep that emotion inside her. When Kyle threatened Sierra more, she felt she had to intervene or Kyle would kill her. "Stop!" Anna said as she stood in front of Kyle. After staring at Anna, Kyle felt something incomprehensible on the inside. "Where's everyone else?" Anna said, holding Kyle's hand as she lowered his gun. "The infected-," Kyle said. he stuttered to speak, as if he was still processing all that had happened to him up to this point.

Kyle eventually managed to speak, "the level five," he stated as he glanced at Sierra and Anna. Kyle was breathing fast, his pulse began beating as he attempted to rise up, and he began going towards his front door to exit the area. "How do I get out?" He stated as he moved towards a shattered ceiling that lifted him to the floor above, "just up ahead," Anna added as she started following him with Sierra, and they both glanced up as they all went up.

Kyle heard a loud shrieking from the top and said, "What was that?!" Kyle murmured as he resumed his run, eyeing him, Sierra and Anna began to follow him as well.

Nate, on the other hand, began killing all the infected he saw along the road, ultimately catching up to one of the crew members, his name was Cole, and they were great friends, "Where's everyone else?" Nate inquired as he approached him, both of them perplexed and concerned about their own lives.

Nate inquired once more, "Where are they?" Nate glanced at Cole and noticed that his hand was seriously bleeding, "The infected-" he whispered slowly, Nate looked at him and found him shivering, "Hey, calm down, what happened?" he questioned as he grabbed him and tried to calm him down, Cole had known Nate for a long time, but it appeared that something was upsetting him "What about those who are infected? I'm going to save everyone! "I'll kill him," Nate screamed angrily, and Cole burst out laughing like a lunatic in a couple of seconds, "You can't kill him." Cole said as he abruptly came to a halt and gave Nate a serious stare. Nate was both confused and concerned about the others. He was surprised when Cole suddenly stopped reacting to him; he instantly grabbed Cole and asked him what was wrong, but there was no response; he eventually understood that Cole had died;

So, he swiftly rolled up Cole's sleeves and discovered a bite mark, thus he hurriedly got up within seconds. Cole turned into an infected in a matter of seconds and immediately attacked Nate, but he was stabbed from behind. "What are you doing here?" John said as he stabbed Cole behind the back. "What are you doing here alone?" Where is everyone else?" In a rage, John glared at Nate......

"Answer me first! Where are the infected?" Nate replied, Nate observed all the wounds on John, who appeared to have been in an intensive struggle...

"Did that infected do this to you?" Nate queried; his gaze fixed on John. "This isn't the time; we need to get out of here immediately," John stated as he began walking forward. "John, tell me what happened in there!" Nate stopped John "We can't stay here; we have to go back," John stated as he began walking by Nate once more. "What about the plan?" Nate remarked this as he grabbed John and stopped him once again. "Don't you realize, it's ridiculous, this plan can't go on any longer," John said as he quickly grabbed Nate's hand and tossed it off his. So, it appeared like John had gone insane as a result of this mission, he persuaded Nate to accompany him as it was the only way to safety "I can't leave, all my crew members need me," Nate explained as he refused John's invitation to join him and abandon the plan, "they are dead!" but we still have a few at the top "John replied.

Kyle, on the other side, was halted at a broken ladder; he took Sierra's help and climbed to the top; he swiftly extended his hand to Anna to help her get up, then helped Sierra; Kyle began examining all the rooftops in search of John or any other survivors, but he was unsuccessful. When John and Nate arrived at the top, they discovered that no one was there. "What in the world is going on? What happened to everyone?" Nate questioned John, who looked at him with uncertainty. John turned around and, happily, saw Anna with Kyle by her side. "Hey, Anna!" He yelled as Nate looked over and found Sierra among them.

The Undead Bonds

Kyle soon recognized John's voice and rushed to approach them, while Sierra and Anna followed Kyle until they reached the roof, where John and Nate awaited them. "Where has everyone gone?" Sierra inquired to John. She spotted Nate and inquired yet again "Where has everyone gone? Please answer!!".

"We have to go NOW," John shouted, interrupting Sierra. She was puzzled "I can't go without my team, and what about our plan? The building is right ahead," Sierra stated, denying what John said, "Where's Aiden?" She inquired...."He was with you!" John replied "And what about Ruthven?"......Kyle fell silent once again, shaking gently and not saying anything.

"Kyle, what happened?" Nate asked, "Are you and Ruthven, okay?" while staring at John and then at Kyle. Anna noticed this and swiftly interrupted the conversation, asking John to come in private since she needed to say something she didn't want others to know.......

"Nate, you already know what happened! Just tell John to stick to the plan "Sierra added, looking at Nate..."No! I believe he is right; our crew members are dead, or so he claims; I am not certain, but I am certain that this location is deadly." Nate responded

Sierra was abruptly seized at gunpoint "John? What?" She remarked this when she noticed John pointing a pistol at her. "Ruthven has died!" Nate's jaw fell, and he instantly looked to Sierra, who, fortunately, nodded her head to Nate. "I warned you that people would die, your crew is dead, and one of our crew members is dead, what else do you need?" As he held his pistol motionless, John stated. "John, pay attention! We can't go back" Sierra stated as he tried to back away from John's pistol......

"Why?" As he walked ahead, John remarked. "The door from which we came is locked," Sierra stated as she stood with her hands in the air. "What exactly do you mean? It's your zone; we're from there." John was perplexed.......

"John, it's too late!"

"What the hell?" Sierra said as Kyle erupted in wrath. "Are you crazy? Sierra, people are dying, ALL YOUR CREW MATES ARE DEAD!" Sierra was silent for a few seconds....... "You had us walk right past our death, and now we're stuck in here!" Kyle said.

Sierra turned to Kyle and John and stated, "Look, the only way we have is to push forward, we've come this far—......

"There's always another way, Sierra!" Kyle cut Sierra off and said. Nate had been quiet for some while, and he kept gazing around for some reason. "What do you think, Nate?" Nate was questioned by John... "Oh, what?" Hewas perplexed...."Nate, what's your plan? Do you want to move ahead or back?" Hewas questioned by John again.

They were abruptly stopped by a loud growling. "Whoa, what was that?" As he peered around for the growling, John asked. "GET OFF ME, YOU-" Someone shrieked in agony and rage. John and everyone else heard the voice as well. "Is that Aiden?" In disbelief, John stated as he began racing towards the sound; everyone else followed John since they were astounded to hear something like that. They hurried down to the streets and heard the loud growling again, but this time it was louder, indicating that they were closing in.

"Through here," John said, and they all stepped inside through a smashed store window of a coffee shop and up the shop's steps.

To their astonishment, they didn't come across a single infected along the way, making their journey both simple and perplexing. They arrived at one of the little destroyed shops on top of the coffee shop.

There was an unnerving hush for a few seconds as John and everyone stood upright looking for the growling and, most crucially, *Aiden*.

EIGHT

The Gordian Knot

Nobody was moving, and there were no infected in sight. "What now?" Sierra stated as she peered around. The huge growl was heard once more during that short silence, and within seconds, the roof of that shop collapsed, and hundreds of infected began to pour. "RUN!" Kyle exclaimed as he leaped down the steps rather than strolling down like a normal person would.

They were all quickly halted when they noticed the coffee shop was also being filled with infected..."Where are we now? We're trapped!" Sierra remarked this as she began shooting at the infected. A big fire was noticed suddenly emanating from the coffee shop. "What is it?" John was taken aback.

They had all spotted a survivor who had ignited a broken stick with a piece of cloth wrapped around the top, similar to a torch. The infected instantly spotted the fire and began focusing on the survivor rather than John and everyone else. The survivor swung his torch around the infected, and it appeared that the infected were afraid of the flames, as they all began to retreat, "Come on, everybody! Hurry!" The survivor remarked this as he cleared a tiny way for them to cross safely.

They all dashed out of the shop and came to a halt behind the retailer's tiny walkway. At long last, the survivor who had saved John and everyone came. He was wearing a mask and a large black jacket around him; he quickly removed his mask, and everyone was surprised to discover the survivor's true face.

"Aiden?"

"Where have you been all this time?" John inquired; his gaze drawn to Aiden. "Everyone, we have to leave!" As he frantically began going forward and backwards, Aiden muttered. He appeared to be under stress..."What happened to you? What was that growling about?" When John noticed Aiden was worried over something, he questioned.

"There's something out there, and it's far larger than the level four infected we faced," Aiden said "Follow me, I have something to show you."

They all immediately began following Aiden without question. Nate was concerned when he heard Aiden describing an infection that was considerably more powerful and terrifying than the level four. His suspicions about the level five infected were gradually confirmed. "Through here, I know a path where we won't come across any infected." Aiden said as he leapt through a wall inside the property. "When we assumed there would be no infected, we were attacked by hundreds." John mentioned

Aiden went through a shattered door into an abandoned house, remaining silent for a few seconds. The house was not large, but it was enough for keeping a family secure. "Everyone, behind this door," Aiden replied, pulling a little key from his pocket and attempting to unlock the door. He opened the door with a creak and unveiled something that surprised everyone.

They all witnessed several helpless survivors who had not been infected but were barely alive and enduring the pandemic. "Sierra!" Aiden spoke slowly "Your crew turned on us,"....

"What do you mean?" Sierra expressed her disbelief and uncertainty. "What's going on, Aiden, and who are they?" In addition, John stated that he was perplexed. "They are Adrien's people," Aiden stated as he glanced at Sierra and pointed to the persons lying on the floor.

They were in poor health and had several wounds on their bodies. "What became of them?" John stated this when he observed them coughing and lying down as if they were about to die. Aiden took a step out of the room and indicated for everyone else to do the same. "They came to you, they were sent by Adrien to obtain medical care, but your people refused to give them anything and instead assaulted them, even I was fired at," Aiden said "What are your true intentions with my brother? And why did they come to you in the first place for medical treatment?"...

"What! That's not possible" Sierra expressed her bewilderment. "Enough now! I spoke with these people, and they told me that everyone from Adrien's side comes to you for medical care on a regular basis; tell us the truth, now!" Aiden stated as he stepped forward gradually, pulling a weapon from his back strap. "Look, there's been a huge misunderstanding," Sierra said...

"What's the matter, Sierra?" John stated this as he and Anna both gazed at her with surprise and wrath... "What was the point of going back with them in the first place unless you were leaving us?" Sierra interrupted as she attempted to divert the subject.

"I encountered other folks on the way who had been assaulted by an enormous infected." After hearing the crucial portion, Aiden murmured as Nate turned to face him. "All of Adrien's guards died, and there were few left; it's my job to help people; this is your only chance to tell the truth."....

"Look, I'll be honest with you, I don't have any-. "STOP LYING," Aiden said as he grew agitated, blasting a bullet on the floor. Aiden was scalding hot, so Sierra took a step back. "You're a liar," he said. Everyone was deafeningly quiet. "GO ON SAY IT, I will give you one last chance," Aiden shouted, threatening Sierra with a genuine shot this time. Anna said after Aiden, "Just say anything now." Sierra was dumbfounded and looked to the left and right before responding, "Alright." This one had everyone's attention.......

"It's a long story, they rescued our team, and you can say that we have the finest doctors in this time of crisis, the first and only reason that kept us alive in their territory was because we were giving them with the best medical care possible, people from Adrien's building comes here every so often to get treated, however the real problem is that they've been considering getting new doctors, leaving us stranded or killing us in the process." Sierra remarked as she looked directly into Aiden's eyes, while others peered at hers. "Do you hear me? They are going to kill us all" Sierra said as her heart skipped a beat and she glanced at everyone. "You have always been a part of him! You were going to betray my brother no matter how awful he had gotten, but what if he's good and it's just you telling us lies about him so we can help you kill him? No matter what happens, I'm not going to have my brother killed by a backstabber" Aiden stated while holding his rifle straight....

"No! You should understand that they will kill us" Sierra stated as she sought to reason with Aiden. "Wake up, Sierra; your own people don't trust you." Aiden yelled at Sierra and afterwards laughed out loud. "Listen, alright, let's do it your way, we'll go visit your brother, and then you can talk to him and-

Aiden cut Sierra and firmly leveled his rifle at her, ready and thrilled to shoot her. As he set his finger on the trigger, they were all distracted by a terrifying growling, which caused Aiden to retract his steps. Nate, on the other hand, was ready to kill the level five infected and immediately left everyone behind to hurry towards the sound coming from the neighboring streets.

Sierra noticed Nate racing towards the exit and immediately ran after him to flee. Aiden was the most horrified of the infected he had previously faced. "Shoot her, Aiden; she's escaping." Voices in Aiden's brain said

He understood what he must do; he hastily pointed his weapon at Sierra and intended to shoot, but his hands began to shake as they all heard the growling once again. "We have to run now," Anna murmured, knowing that the infected were nearby and may strike at any time. The growling grew louder and louder. "Aiden, if you don't shoot, I will," John stated as he took out his rifle and aimed at Sierra. He tried to press the trigger but was quickly disarmed by Aiden. "Don't shoot," he urged as he gripped John's hand and withdrew his rifle. "Aiden! WHY?" As he and everyone else watched Sierra walk through the door with Nate, John said...

"John, we must save the people who are inside first; we can't face this infected," Aiden stated as he turned swiftly and began opening the door.

"Hey! What do you mean, Aiden?" John was perplexed, but he agreed. Anna was terrified after hearing the growling twice, therefore she gingerly pulled out her pistol in case of an emergency and began glancing around her. Kyle was mystified; he stood there, unsure of what was going on, and appeared to be lost in contemplation.

Kyle, don't just stay quiet; help us! Aiden stated as he and John began pushing survivors on the ground to safety. Kyle still appeared to be disoriented, but after a few seconds, he was back to normal and raced directly to the survivors who required help.

Anna stood back and held her weapon straight. Kyle instinctively put the survivors' hand on his shoulder and began walking behind John and Aiden. He suddenly noticed a little mark on the survivor's neck and shoved him, presuming it was a bite mark from an infected. The survivor was shoved down with a loud thud. "Ow Fu-" the survivor muttered as he began to groan. Anna took a step back with a tiny gasp, she still had lot going through her head, but she tried to remain strong. "What happened? KYLE?" John strained to turn back and see since he was carrying two survivors by himself. "He's infected!" Kyle yelled as he slumped from terror. John was stunned, while Anna became even more terrified

"What are you talking about?" Aiden voiced his surprise at hearing this. Kyle snatched the survivor's collar and rolled it down to reveal his neck. There was, definitely, a bite mark. "He's bitten," Kyle shouted as he shoved him away. John and Aiden swiftly relaxed the survivors and spotted the bite mark themselves. They saw the survivor slowly deteriorate into an infected. "Anna, hold on!" John yelled as he raced up to her and stood in front of her.

"John! We have bigger issues; these survivors have also been bitten" Aiden stated as he inspected the necks of all the survivors who they were helping. Kyle quickly returned to the room and learned that the virus had infected all of the other survivors.

"Quickly step back, they're all infected," Kyle said, leading and urging John, Aiden, and Anna to exit the home. They all dashed out and were instantly hunted by the infected survivors. "HEY! Through this" As he shattered the glass and leapt through it, Aiden screamed. The infected were hampered but did not cease following them. Kyle was the last to jump, and so as he attempted to leap through the window, he was grabbed from behind by one of the infected. "Kyle! Hold on!" As he shot the infected, John told Kyle to keep going. They were halted immediately following the Kyle incident because there were so many streets heading in different directions that they were disoriented. "Where are we going now?" Kyle inquired as he glanced all the streets, some of which were partially blocked and others were obstructed by barricades and wrecked vehicles.

Aiden marked out a path, and they all began moving in that direction, accompanying Aiden. The path led them to an abandoned train station. They leaped the gates and proceeded directly to the station office, but as when they arrived, they were met by a swarm of infected inside. Aiden stated, "We can't move through here," as he noticed the infected blocking the door. "Hold on!" Kyle stated as he pulled one of the iron shelves and flung it towards the infected.

Some of the infected were trapped, while many were able to escape. Kyle saw the opportunity and shot repeatedly on all the infected to open their path. They all traversed doors after doors till they came to a halt. They all sat on a rusted seat alongside a derailed railroad.

"What should we do now?" Kyle inquired as he tried to catch his breath and unwind.

"We should go back," John continued, however he was cut off by Aiden. "It's blocked; Sierra's men have barred them and are shooting at anyone who tries to enter," Aiden explained "Our only option is to go to the tower and talk to my brother." Aiden had concluded that the sole route he wanted to travel was to the building, also known as "Adrien's Tower."....

But, Anna stammered as she looked at Aiden. "What about Sierra and Nate?" She inquired; her eyes wide with uncertainty. "Why are you worried about her?" Aiden stated that he was still enraged with Sierra since she was the one who planned everything and then betrayed them. "NO!" consider this: all of the survivors sent to Sierra's camp were bitten and infected, WHY?" Anna indicated that she suspected that there was something amiss. "Wait, she has a point, why would Adrien send infected survivors to Sierra's camp?" John replied, agreeing with Anna but also perplexed.

"Not only that, but did you notice that all of the infected survivors were bitten on the neck?" Anna said, making a critical observation.

Kyle was immersed in thoughts at this juncture, and everyone sensed that there was something wrong. "Look, I'm telling you again, no matter what, the only possible option we have is to Adrien's tower," Aiden stated decisively as he rose up with his rifle, ready to slay any infected out there. "Are you sure? Perhaps we can try something else-

Anna stated this before being cut short by John. "Anna, he's right, we need to get to the building," John remarked, pausing Anna and supporting Aiden's next action by standing up with him.

Anna turned at Kyle, expecting another response, but Kyle, too, backed Aiden and John and stood up with them.

Anna was dismayed by this conclusion, but as she threw a glance towards John, she felt better. "Trust me, Anna, everything will work out!" As he held her hand, John told Anna to mark each word. The crew was finally ready, and they were all heading forward with their hearts racing. They cautiously entered the shattered train that was not on the tracks, but as they advanced, Anna noticed a disruption and began to get bad feelings surrounding her. She kept stopping in the middle of the route and was sometimes slower compared to the others.

"Anna, what happened?" John inquired as he became anxious about her. Anna had no clue what was going on as she waddled normally but fainted unlooked. "Hey, Anna, wake up!" As he held the fainting Anna in his hands, John said. As He panicked, Aiden turned back and questioned what happened to Anna, to which John answered, "I'm not sure, give me a water bottle."

Kyle hurriedly dug inside his backpack and handed John a bottle of water; John swiftly removed the lid and dumped the bottle over Anna's face. Anna gasped and awakened; she glanced around and was slowly questioned by John, "Are you okay?" Anna was feeling nauseated, and she didn't say anything for a few seconds prior to actually saying that she was OK. She began to have difficulties walking, so John offered her his shoulder; she took John's help and continued walking slowly with John along her side.

After passing through some doors on the train, they all arrived at a compartment where they saw several infected on the seats, but they weren't yet awake.

"Should we shoot them?" Kyle pondered, believing that killing them was the ultimate choice. "Is it necessary? Anna isn't feeling well right now, so I don't believe it's worth the risk "As he rejected Kyle's suggestion, John added...

"We should go through, we are low on supplies, I lost all the supplies, plus I think you could be forgetting a few things to go with this plan, there are a lot of bags and luggage of these people, maybe we should grab those first" Aiden stated as he scrutinized the luggage of the dead travelers who had become infected. "Take the supplies, but be very quiet," John said as he concurred with Aiden that they were running low on supplies. Kyle and Aiden exchanged glances and devised a strategy. Kyle carefully sat down and discreetly laid on his chest, hastily but softly pushing himself and attempting to collect all the briefcases and luggage from which many goods were scattered on the surface. Kyle went for the opposite side of the compartment; it appeared that their main objective was to take everything from the top compartment.

Kyle gradually began grabbing as much bags as he could, focusing on the larger bags first since they were more likely to contain a huge number of essential items. He began taking out each thing from the bag one at a time and slipping them to Aiden while remaining completely silent. Aiden and John were grabbing everything and shoving it into their backpacks. "How much is it now? We already have enough, and we don't need more" As he saw that all the bags were filled and there was no more space for anything, John murmured quietly to Aiden.

"Just a little more, John, and we'll be on our way," Aiden remarked, putting more items into an already stuffed backpack....

"Okay, stop, that's enough," John exclaimed as he noticed that the backpack had reached its capacity, but Aiden was still attempting to stuff more and more items inside.

Kyle, on the other hand, spotted them and instantly tried to calm them down since there were infected all around them who may wake up and target them, but he failed terribly because he couldn't yell and had to whisper. "John-" Anna said quietly before collapsing again. "Shit! Anna! Hey! Hey!" John was taken aback when he turned around and grabbed Anna. "Aiden, we must go quickly."

Kyle noticed Anna fainting and John clutching her, he quickly stood up and with a dismayed stare. he turned around and began opening the door, he tried to unlock the door but struggled, he whereupon noticed an emergency hammer box however he failed to realize that all the infected were surrounding him as he quickly took and hammer out and smashed the glass of the window, this induced all the infected to panic. John and Aiden were likewise unaware of what was going on; as soon as they spotted the glass cracking, they witnessed all of the infected waking up and losing their wits.

As Kyle turned around, he spotted the infected swarming around him and also attempting to open the door through which he had entered. John grabbed Anna and began fleeing as Aiden kept the infected back. "Just lock the door on the next compartment". As they rushed towards the compartment opposite Kyle's, John mutters to Aiden.

Few moments later

Sierra and Nate huddled behind a giant rock. "Look, we can work on this!" Nate attempted to respond but was cut off by one of the survivors at the gate. It appeared like Sierra and Nate tried to return to their base but were met by weapons all around them.

"Listen, it's not worth talking to them, Aiden was correct over them, we have to kill each one or flee, our alternatives are limited," Sierra remarked to Nate....

"Look, I agree, but we need that weapon or we won't have a chance out there," Nate continued to yell at the survivors on the gate. "But what's the point?" Sierra said "But we can't go in there, nor we can't go back to John and his crew; everywhere we go, we'll be killed, so it's pointless."

Nate was dubious and angry, but he knew what he was doing was crucial for survival. Sierra was having none of it; she was anxious and terrified to fight because they were so few in number. "Hey, just stop- Sierra tried to clutch Nate's hand but was quickly flung off by Nate. "Shut up, I know you lied," Nate said, looking at Sierra with disappointment......

"What? What exactly do you mean?" Sierra expressed her perplexity. "You never planned to kill Adrien because you wanted to protect your people's lives," Nate said, taking his gaze away from her. "Of course, I planned to save them," Sierra responded, rejecting Nate's objection. "Here it is again, lies, you intended to kill Adrien in order to become the ruler of the entire city," Nate said as he checked the rounds in his pistol. Sierra was stunned; she realized she couldn't lie any longer and had no choice but to come clean. "How do you know?" she questioned; her voice quiet but assured. "It doesn't matter; I know a way for us to live," Nate said "We can kill Adrien quickly and easily, even John."

Sierra first denied the statements, but Nate persisted. "That's the only way we have, you won't be able to survive alone for long," Nate attempted to persuade her. Nate began silently packing his guns while Sierra suffered some setbacks. "What's the plan?" she said as she decided to join Nate on their mission for survival.

"We surrender"

Sierra was in disbelief, she contradicted Nate several times, and despite this, Nate still warned Sierra to stick to his plan or they would both perish. They both packed combustible weapons and tucked blades beneath their shoes and sleeves. "Follow me," Nate urged as he and Sierra moved out of the cover, hands in the air. "So you finally give up," the survivor remarked, laughing out loud. Sierra was filled with rage. "You can't command us anymore, Sierra," the survivor stated as he trash talked Sierra till she snapped and shot the trash talking survivor. "What the hell, Sierra?" Nate shouted as they dashed into the tent.

As expected, they were apprehended in a matter of seconds and subsequently sent to bars. "That part wasn't necessary," Nate muttered as he and Sierra walked together, their wrists shackled behind their backs. "I had to show them that I am not one of their kind," Sierra said firmly as she went through the door. They were later imprisoned with two other survivors. "What the heck," Jack said, astonished and mystified to find Sierra in the imprisonment despite the fact that she was the group's leader. "What exactly is she doing here?" As Jack and Sierra established an unexpected eye contact, he murmured to Nate......"Do you know who these men are?" Sierra inquired, astounded that those two knew who Nate is. "I know," He said. "Did you bring what I asked?"

Nate swiftly crept to him since he was bound and his legs were chained. Slowly, he approached Kim and pulled a key from his boots. "Opposite the medical area and behind the bars," Kim said as Sierra looked on, perplexed. Nate crept cautiously and attempted to release Jack and Kim's shackles using a novel approach.

They were all imprisoned in a tiny room that was covered with sheets and broken wall pipes. They appeared to have been placed just beneath a water plant, since there was water trickling from the top. "When did you plan everything there?" Sierra inquired as she watched Nate describe something she had no idea had happened. "So they both were with you the entire time?" Sierra queried...."They were," Nate answered with a serious expression and a theatrical smile. He unfastened Sierra's cuffs and set everyone free. Sierra's botched strategy had left insufficient survivors to defend all of the locations. As a result, their way was unblocked and Nate and others could easily cross it. They ascended the ladders and peered out to inspect the surroundings. "Did you see anything?" Sierra inquired while she waited. "There are two up front," Nate said....

"What do you think? Should we eliminate them?" Sierra inquired to Nate. "We need weapons," Nate said, figuring that having guns would give them an advantage.

"Got it, follow me," Sierra responded, preparing to go back inside the prison route. "What are you doing?" Kim inquired, perplexed after watching Sierra return inside. Sierra remained mute for several seconds before saying, "Take whatever you need."

She carefully opened a door, revealing a slew of weaponry and supplies. "Did you keep this a secret the whole time?" Kim stated as he looked up, puzzled, while Nate stood frozen, despite the fact that he, too, had no idea about the gun safe. They were all loaded up in a matter of seconds. There were a bunch of survivors camped near the front gate a few blocks away from this prison. They were all laughing until one of them abruptly turned around. "What happened to you all of a sudden?" the survivor inquired to the other survivor.

He began strolling slowly towards the prison, feeling he heard something from that direction. When he arrived, he was greeted with a large pistol in the head. "Sierra? What happened! Please do not shoot! I beg you! I didn't do anything wrong." The survivor spoke in a fearful and cryptic tone. "Look, don't try to act innocent," Sierra urged, drawing the gun closer to the survivor's head. "What? NO! What do you mean?!" As he stood there with his hand in the air, the survivor stammered once more to speak. "Wait, Sierra! They aren't with those survivors who tossed us here," Nate added, leaning closer and whispering.

"What do you mean?" Sierra replied in hushed tones, having no clue what Nate was on about. "What I'm trying to say is that you're still their leader for these people, but there were a few survivors who loathed you, so they put us in this filthy place so that they can all dominate the whole group," Nate explained as Sierra lowered her weapon and walked confidently outdoors. Everyone else began to follow her, and they all arrived at the spot where Nate was headed.

Sierra saw her tent, suggested Nate join her, and rushed inside without further ado. Nate noticed her sprinting and tried to call her, but she continued going, thus Nate decided to carry on his journey alone with Jack and Kim.

Sierra stepped inside and the first thing she noticed was her photo on the bed; she picked it up and found her mother's side was burned; she had treasured this photo since it was the only photo she had with her family. "Sierra? What are you doing?" An old lady appeared out of nowhere and questioned. "I am here for some work" Sierra replied back with jitter. The lady walked in closer and said "So you did execute the plan and let me think-

"You lost"

Sierra took a step back and gasped, but she didn't turn around to face the lady.... "We'll win, we're so close," Sierra enthused as she quickly began packing all of the items. "Then why did you come here- all alone? As she approached and mumbled in her ears, the lady inquired. "No, no, no, I came here with my team." Sierra stuttered and turned around to find herself alone; she looked about rapidly but saw no one; she felt dizzy; even the lady had vanished into thin air or she wasn't here at all.

Nate dashed into what appeared to be a bunker beneath the infected jail; as soon as he got through the red-colored entrance, he took out his key and promptly opened a little box that lay just in front of him. He heard an infected behind him as he retrieved the documents and several lab bottles from the box, however he kept filling his bag with lab bottles and scrutinizing them. He then saw a bottle labeled "SOUTHEN LAB BIOTECH."

He immediately grabbed it and was ready to escape when he noticed an infected blocking his path. He was a touch low in stature and appeared to be a mid-aged adolescent kid, but Nate didn't see him as a threat and began running with a gun in his hand.

"Come on, Nate, move faster!" He grunted as he tried to rush things as fast as he could while whacking the infected away, but as soon as he got close, he halted in surprise, "What? - It was Mike, and Nate was stunned. He hesitated to shoot him, and his heart began to race since he was already in a panic and tense. He attempted to flee as quickly as he possibly could, leaving his misgivings behind. Nate appeared to recognize Mike.

"But how?"

NINE

Moribund

"What exactly is it, Aiden?" John inquired as he studied something heavy on Anna's messed-up leg. Anna was drenched in sweat. "It's the infection," Aiden stated as he examined the infection on Anna's leg and spotted it moving on its own. John grabbed some cloths and cautiously tried to remove the infection. "This looks horrible," Kyle commented as he saw the sticky stuff being taken from Anna's leg. John grabbed the infection and hurled it away as quickly as he could.......

"How are you feeling now, Anna?" John inquired as he handed her some water, while she tried to steady herself by holding John.

Anna sipped the water slowly and soon said to keep going. "What? Have you gone insane, Anna? You're not in any shape to keep moving," John replied as Aiden calmed him down. "We have to keep going, John,"

Kyle remarked "Who knows what Sierra is up to?"

"No! Anna is in no position to move," John said, softly helping Anna to sit. "Kyle, we should wait as Anna needs our help," Aiden said, glancing down at the dead infection on the floor. "See, we can carry her-".

"SHUT UP, DUMB IDIOT!"...

"Please hear me out! Please. Ruthven is dead, and I blame Sierra," Kyle stated....

"Kyle, you're not making any sense," John replied while Anna observed John's racing heart and tried to say something but was cut off by her puking. She felt woozy, and her eyes began to roll up, causing her to lose control. "Anna, can you hear me?" John yelled as he tried to rouse Anna awake by gently hitting her, but she didn't respond. She was having hallucinations. She pictured herself standing with a bloody knife in her hand, and on the floor was a lady who had been stabbed to death, the same person Sierra encountered. Anna was weeping, her heartbeat quickened as she began to breathe deeply, and she felt terrified and hopeless as she gazed at the body. It was difficult for her to continue staring at her, but she did so nonetheless, the knife in her hand falling as she stood by her knees sobbed.

She carefully retracted the knife and prepared to stab herself, but she was unable to do it. She began weeping harder and attempted to swing the knife again, but it accidentally wounded her leg.

She didn't realize she was locked in a cycle of regretting her killing the lady, and she didn't stop. "John! The leg," Aiden exclaimed, as John comprehended the situation but blanked when Aiden told him to take out the infection, which would cause Anna excruciating agony. "I'll do it," Kyle responded as he took a step forward.......
"No, not you," John said, softly pushing him. "What's the problem, John?" Kyle expressed his disbelief. "I'll do it, she's my responsibility," John said as he swiped the knife over the infection, causing a large amount of blood to come out. Aiden took a rug from his backpack and applied rubbing alcohol to Anna's leg before attaching the rug to her leg.

He covered her minor cut and scratches as Anna screamed in her dreams when she awoke. "What was going on with me?" Anna pondered, looking around and realizing they had left the railway station a long time ago. "It's the infection, when the infected dies, a part of their body from where they got infected doesn't quite die," Aiden explained.

"If I got bit by an infected in my hand, I would turn like them, and even if you decided to kill me, a part of my hand would stay alive and look just like this, and I would still have the power to infect anyone." Aiden pointed to the infection that had been removed..."But what happened to her, Aiden? She wasn't even conscious!" As he held Anna in his hands, John inquired to Aiden. "When you catch it, it attempts to control your brain and makes you remember your darkest memories and makes you revisit it, making you numb and paralyzed in order to kill you".

"Like a loop," John said.

"That's right, a loop."

Anna understood something and questioned Aiden, "Am I going to turn?" as she stammered in pain. "Hopefully not," Aiden said. "We took the infected from you; this infection takes twenty-four hours to turn someone"...... "Was I going to have to live through what I just witnessed for the next twenty-four hours?" Anna wondered, picturing Aiden with a terrified expression. "Sadly, yeah," Aiden said as he cleansed her wounds once again. She looked down at her leg and attempted to move; she nearly lifted her leg but failed. John advised Anna not to try and move her leg.

He gradually helped her in walking; they were barely able to cover some distance, so Kyle began to accompany them as well; Aiden in front cleared their area. He blasted one of the locks that was obstructing a large corridor leading to an elevator. He tried to open the door, and when he did, he found that the elevator was stuck at the top. "How do we get up?" Kyle inquired as he tried to press the elevator's button but received no response. Aiden advised that they keep looking for another path because the infected had already run over most of the areas.

Kyle jumped onto the cable that was barely keeping the elevator up. "What are you doing, Kyle?" As Kyle attempted to climb to the top, John screamed. The elevator was making a strange noise. Kyle looked up and knew there was a problem. "No! No! No!" yelled John as the bottom of the elevator broke out, sending waves of water all over the area.

Within minutes, the floors began to crumble and flooded with the water at the bottom. Unfortunately, Kyle lost his balance as the flow of water dropped directly on his face with pressure, creating a big puddle at the bottom that was still overflowing. "We need to jump," Anna stated, as John immediately opposed and pleaded for another route down. "John! "They're all coming," Anna remarked, explaining that she has visions of where the infection is spreading.

"How is that possible?"

"It is possible John, she was ready to get infected, I feel like it's working". Aiden stated as Anna looked perplexed, however she was able to walk without pain. Big waves pushed them far out, and they all tried to steady themselves by holding onto anything they could find.

Kyle was well ahead, rolling up and down till he was called. "Hey kiddo, give me your hand," the survivor yelled as he tried to pull him up. Kyle quickly took his hand and climbed up, turning around since he knew John and everyone else were still following him due to the tremendous flow of water. "Hey! There are others with me; please help me in saving them" Kyle stated as he looked around but saw no one. "What the hell happened to them?" Kyle was agitated and prepared to re-enter from the opposite side.

But the survivor stopped him just as he was ready to leap. "What in the world are you doing?" As he grabbed him from behind, he shouted. Suddenly, John and Anna appeared, followed by Aiden in the back. Kyle grabbed John's hand, while the survivor took Aiden's as they both climbed, John grabbed Anna and pulled her.

"Aiden Hart?"

Aiden made direct eye contact with the survivor, as if they knew each other. "Patrick? YOU?" Aiden inquired, smiling and glancing at his boyhood buddy. "It definitely is, man," Patrick said as they both hugged... "What are you doing here? I'm sure I can help you if you need it." Patrick told Aiden that seeing his old friend made his eyes wet...."Well, sure, we do need your help," Aiden responded, looking at John and Anna. He didn't ask many questions. "We need to get to the building," John told the survivor. "What? No, Why?" Patrick inquired, stumbling in shock. "Patrick? My brother, I want to meet him," Aiden said, asking Patrick to take them there. "I'm sure I can help, no doubt about that, but-

"But what"

"It's impossible"

The Undead Bonds

"What do you mean, Patrick?" Aiden inquired, perplexed. "It's pointless Aiden, but if you insist, I must accompany you there," Patrick said, dodging the suspicious gaze. "But is he there? Adrien, my brother?" Aiden inquired to Patrick, hoping to discover more about his brother. "Uh- um- Yea- Yeah!" Patrick looked timid, while Aiden looked bewildered. "Take us there," Aiden asked Patrick, who agreed because the path was only a few minutes away.

They all started walking uphill, passing a few dead infected bodies along the way. To lighten the situation, Patrick tried to strike up a little chat with his buddy. "Now, Aiden, I remember you once told me you had a dog," Patrick remarked as he walked through a fenced-in area, unlocked a door with the key he possessed... "I used to, Patrick, why do you inquire?" Aiden replied while smiling and looking at Patrick, who was now overjoyed to finally talk about dogs. Prior to the apocalypse, Patrick ran an animal shelter for dogs and cats, but he preferred dogs over cats, and he used to adopt almost any single dog that others didn't want so that those left dogs could also experience love and care with a roof over their heads...."My dog misses your dog and even you ha-ha-ha," Patrick said with a goofy grin. Aiden left the conversation and continued walking after that. They all came to a tall building in front of them, which was undoubtedly Adrien's tower. "This is it, brother," Patrick said "I can't go in, but you certainly can."

"Patrick? What's the problem? You're acting strange and confusing us "Aiden inquired, gently punching his shoulder. "Go, Aiden, don't question me! Now!" Patrick responded as he pushed Aiden inside the building. John took Anna without hesitation, and the closest buddies were finally separated. Patrick took his own path.

He returned, and just as he was ready to leap back in, He observed some survivors yelling for help.

He dashed closer to them, noticing a woman and a man who were nearly run over by hordes of infected. Patrick landed a couple hard hits on the infected as he hurried to them for rescue...... "Here! Please follow me "As he cleared the way for them, Patrick remarked. "Thank you," Sierra said. It was undoubtedly Nate and Sierra although Nate was disguised by a black cloak and a grey mask. When Patrick looked at Nate, he appeared to recognize him, although not exactly because of the disguise..."We should keep going, Nate," Sierra stated as they set off on their route. Patrick simply sat there, terrified, after witnessing Nate and Sierra go.

"Boss!" Patrick remarked

John was exhausted, he had been holding Anna for a long time, they were climbing stairs after stairs, the entire building appeared to be vacant, all the rooms they entered were filled but no one could be seen, all the chairs, bed, and hall appeared to be empty. They were all confused until they came across a room with a noise inside that was shut, and they all concluded that they had finally discovered someone in this building.

Aiden took a step forward and banged on the door. "HEY!" He repeated it as he continued to bang on the door till, Kyle proposed, "Let's destroy it," to which Aiden answered, "GO ON! The door is all yours."

Kyle launched a few decent pushes but failed each time.

"You finally did make yourself look like a clown," Aiden quipped as he moved to push the door but was thwarted by Anna, who stepped up and kicked the door, shattering it in a single stroke.

Everyone stepped in without questions; they were astonished to find Anna with such a huge force; Aiden was anxious; he knew something was wrong, and it was all because of the infected, or so he assumed.

Anna was the first to enter, followed by John, Kyle, and Aiden, who were taken aback when they discovered a TV airing a show. "So that's where the noise was coming from," Aiden said as he switched off the television. Kyle was going to turn around when all of a sudden, *"Look out"*

Someone smacked Kyle in the stomach. "HEYY! What the Fu*k!" said John as he tried to strike the survivor. The survivor dodged all of the punches, and to no surprise, John was able to dodge all of the survivor's strikes, until the survivor eventually got some decent blows, but John had not been in excellent shape from the start, so he was visibly out of form. Aiden entered the battle by aiming a gun at the survivor, but Kyle abruptly seized the pistol from Aiden; they both wrestled, but Kyle fired the bullet. The bullet missed the survivor since it was difficult to even grasp the pistol properly. The survivor swiftly attempted to kick Kyle's hand, but John grabbed the survivor from behind. The survivor was wearing thick gear, but John and others were able to successfully snap the survivor's face mask off. ***It was a girl....***"Who are you?" John questioned, gripping her hard.

"None of your business," she yelled as she struggled to break free from John's grip... "Do you understand what you've done?" John retorted angrily. The girl fought to get free, while Kyle, who was in severe agony, rose up in wrath and terror. "I will kill you," he said, pulling a pistol from his weapon strap. He raced fiercely towards her and attempted to kill her, but was halted by Aiden....

"Wait, there's no need to kill her," Aiden said. "She seems young, Kid, how old are you?"...

"Okay, why do you care?" she said, with a furious expression on her face.

She tried to hit John again, however this time she failed. John had had enough of her, so he interlocked her legs with his, causing her to tumble on the ground, then he seized both of her hands and tied them together with a cloth. "Leave me alone!" She shouted again and even attempted to untie herself, but John would not let her go. "We need to ask some questions, then we promise we'll let you go," John stated as he tried to calm her down. "Just get off of me," she demanded.

There was a lot of struggling and fighting, so Aiden decided to put an end to it. They needed answers, and she was the one who may be capable of helping them, therefore Aiden went up and smashed his weapon across her head, knocking her unconscious.

After fifteen minutes, John stood up, hauled her up, and tied her to the chair. He then took a bottle of water and splashed some water in her eyes, causing her to wake up in horror. "What!! What have you done?" She screamed as she realized she was trapped and struggled to get free.......

"No need to move, kid, it's OK," John remarked as he stood in front of her, expressionless. "My name is Aiden Hart, nice to meet you," Aiden said as he proceeded to shake her hand. The girl spotted him and stopped moving; she appeared exhausted and incapable of moving for long. "It's okay, we're not your enemy, we just need some answers," Aiden spoke again, and so this time she looked back at him before facing down.

"Aiden Hart?" She spoke

"Do you know who my brother is? What about Adrien Hart?" Aiden questioned her; his eyes full of hope for a reunion with his brother. The girl stayed closed, she slowly glanced down and dropped eye contact with Aiden, she began whimpering, and noticing this, John arose, kneeled down, and asked her what happened. Suddenly, sluggish footsteps were heard from outside, but no one noticed because everyone was focused on the girl......."Everyone get out of here!" Nate said, aiming a gun at their heads; Sierra followed her, also armed, and aimed her rifle at them.

It happened all at once for John and everyone; as soon as they realized someone had entered the room, they pulled out their weapons and prepared to battle without even knowing who had arrived. They eventually realized it was Nate and Sierra. "Sierra and Nate, it's four against two, you can't win," John stated as the four were prepared to fight. "That's where you screw up," Nate replied with a little smile, the girl in the back stood behind Aiden with a gun, she had broken free and was now in tip top shape..."Look, John, we're not here to fight; we just need her; if you do something stupid, you die," Nate stated as the girl slowly began to move, her pistol still up. Nate and Sierra left the room, and the girl followed. As she was leaving, she turned around and looked at Aiden one more time, sobbing, and whispered, *"I'm sorry."*

Aiden observed the sadness in her eyes but didn't understand what was going on. "What about that girl? What is her relation with Nate?" Aiden said "And why can't I figure anything out about my brother?". "Aiden, listen to me, something is wrong, but we must follow Nate; who knows what secrets this building holds but Nate does, No, he knows something we don't." Aiden noticed the intensity in John's eyes as he spoke.

He and Kyle decided to follow them. After exiting the room and seeing no one, John instantly discovered some steps and began climbing. He came upon a little note on the ground that said

Climb two more stairs without opening any doors; when you reach the third, unlock the fourth door or you will perish.

When John passed this note to Aiden, he replied, "This could have been left by the girl." John was unsure, and he was both uncomfortable and perplexed. "It's simple, John; all we have to do is follow what this letter says." Kyle spoke while John stood motionless. "What happened to you?" Aiden followed.

"There are no steps," John stated to Aiden and Kyle.

They were all taken aback when they saw there were no staircases. "It must have been a joke," Kyle remarked, dismissing the note as useless. "What if it isn't? Nate, Sierra, and that other girl? Did they vanish into thin air? Something is going on in this building, and we need to figure out what it is" As he made his final step on the next floor, John remarked. Everyone was pleased by John's decision as they followed him; they all noted the entire floor was filled with nothingness and various types of doors.

The entire rectangle was covered with doors with no notion what may be behind them. Aiden flung the note as they approached the floor to inspect it, but there was a line behind it that they missed, ***"don't say a thing or they will kill you"***

Anna began to feel uneasy as she walked a few steps; John observed this and swiftly approached her, asking, "Are you okay?" Anna felt dizzy as well, thus she drank some water.

"God knows how many infected are in this building!" It's messing with my head," Anna said as Aiden finally confirmed that the infection that attacked Anna was able to complete his task. "Will she turn? Aiden!" While staring into Aiden's eyes, John's heartbeat quickened, and when he looked at Anna, she also appeared worried.......

"I don't believe so, the infection takes twenty-four hours, as I mentioned, but in her case, it's something different, it seemed like her body had accepted the infection, you could say she's immune, but no, she can use all the abilities that an infected can use, this doesn't explain it no" As Aiden was deep in thought, he remarked......

"I'm not sensing any changes in my body, but it appears that something is there in me; it's not bothering me, but it has altered me," Anna responded, looking at Aiden with dismay. "Guys!" Aiden was suspicious, "it's not the right moment!"

Kyle was having difficulty accepting what was going on around him, thus he ordered everyone to stay quiet. Everyone was perplexed, but Anna wanted to say something, however John promptly placed his palm over her mouth. All the doors were being slammed from the other side, it appeared that people were stranded and wanted to exit the room, the place was already covered with dozens of doors and there was nowhere further to go, the pounding became louder.

"You should have gone while you had the chance."

Nate was standing directly on top of them on a wooden board erected between two pillars as the voice came from above. "We knew you'd follow us, so I would like to offer you a present for making the worst mistake of your life," Nate remarked as Sierra and the girl stood by his side.

Aiden spotted the girl, who was upset, but she began to say something, however just before Aiden understood her, **"RELEASE THEM!"** The doors were blasted out, and the infected ran; nevertheless, one door remained closed and silent. Everyone began firing as if they were in a war. Anna began punching every infected that came in her path. Aiden was still trying to decipher what that girl was saying since he knew she was striving to help them in escaping this trap.

The girl's signals were constantly getting blocked by infected, the hordes continued rushing in, and Aiden was fighting to find a method to contact the girl,

Therefore, when the girl realized Aiden couldn't grasp what she was doing, she pointed to a door that was still shut. Aiden observed the sign, and the girl immediately tried to warn him to stay away from there, but Nate noticed Aiden gazing at the girl, so He shoved the girl behind his back. Unfortunately for Aiden, he did not notice the warning sign. He kept fighting the hordes of infected in order to clear the passage as quickly as possible and then flee this madness. Another thing to notice is that the path they came from was closed by Nate when he released the infected, leaving them with no choice except to fight the infected.

Anna had reached her limit; she had defeated more infected than anybody else; if it hadn't been for Anna, everyone would have died. Nate observed Anna battling the infected like an expert, he realized something and immediately leapt off the wooden board, he went into a tiny cabinet behind him, and there were several guys who Nate ordered to retrieve Anna and bring her straight to Nate. The entire group had eventually defeated the infected, as they all breathed a sigh of relief, but they knew it wasn't over since they hadn't seen Nate while they looked around.

Aiden, on the other hand, was on the verge of collapsing but managed to stay upright. "You believe it's all over." Several guys arrived, carrying large red and black body amour and staring rifles.

Anna spotted these men and promptly attacked them, but she had no idea that these guys had just arrived to fetch her. One of the survivors, "The hunter," was the most powerful human-infected.

He battled Anna with ease and didn't stop until she was out of breath. He grabbed her and carried her over to Nate. Everyone tried to assault the men, but all of their shots were reflected due to the armor they donned. Nate led Anna to a separate floor, accompanied by Hunter and Sierra. The girl dashed up to Aiden and John's group to aid them; they were all fatigued, but it wasn't finished yet; the girl wasted no time and yelled, "We must leave now! FAST!" They all heard her but only managed to move a short distance before hearing another loud bang...."Where do you all think you're going?" Hunter stated as the final remaining door was finally opened, revealing the most deadly and massive creature they had ever seen in their lives.

TEN

The Level Five

Everyone was stunned to witness the huge infected any human had ever seen, encased in shackles that were attempting to contain the infected. "Oh God," the girl exclaimed as she continued to push Aiden up and force him to stand on his legs. "Is this what a level five looks like?" With a shocked expression, John muttered as he glanced at the infected. The girl took a step forward, saying she would try to keep the infected in place. The infected was therefore wrapped by electric rings to keep him contained in this post-apocalyptic world. The girl pulled out her nun chucks. "Do you honestly believe this will make a difference?" While glancing at the girl's weapon choice, John commented.

"You're in no shape to fight and kill someone like him; it's impossible, but we have to try," the girl remarked as she smiled at John.

When John witnessed that smile, he had a flashback of Sally and Mike on their summer vacation on a beach, Sally running to John, calling him "Dad," and falling directly into the hole created by Mike. Both of them laughed. John was a fantastic surfer by passion, and he used to teach Sally how to surf since she liked it and had made it her hobby.

Mike, on the other hand, was interested in beach volleyball and would join random individuals to play when John taught Sally how to surf.

One day, all of a sudden, Daisy told John on the phone, "I can't deal with this anymore."

"What do you mean, Daisy?" John stated "We have kids." Daisy cried out on the phone, but horrible fate befell John. A few days later, John receives a phone call from Daisy's mother. "Hello?" As he answers the phone, John said.

"I am Daisy's mother," she says on the phone, her tone somber as she sobs. "Are you all right? What happened?" Suddenly his pulse rate increased and his breathing rate went up, John remarked...."She's dead" The mother said as John burst out screaming while his phone fell to the ground. Mike and Sally noticed their father, but as they glanced at him, he was out of control, shattering everything, so Mike and Sally fled to their room, terrified as John watched his kid running away from him.

He knew that everything had fallen apart; he sobbed on the ground, and the family was grieved once John learned of his wife's death.

Mike and Sally sat on their bed, wrapping the blanket around them, turning out the lights and closing the door. John quickly drove down to a nearby bar and waited there till he was caught passed out in the morning. Mike and Sally had been up all night, not knowing where their father was or that their mother had died. They waited until the morning before they heard a cop siren outside their house, during which point Mike and Sally dashed out, only to find their father in terrible health. John was no longer inebriated, and seeing his children outside staring at him made him regret his choices.

He sat down with his children and had a chat about their mother and John's wife Daisy. He tried to explain in a gental way, but the kids were nevertheless devastated to learn of their mother's death, as who wouldn't be? John was upset because he had no understanding what was going on.

Mike hurried to his room and closed the door, however Sally walked up to john and hugged him firmly, saying, "Dad, don't worry, I'm with you." She said, "YOU have us, don't worry," with a little smile. Years later, John witnessed the same smile.

Returning in the present, John was finally conscious, and out of his flashbacks, he observed the girl attempting to entice the level five to her, along with Aiden and Kyle, who were attempting to shoot the infected. John sprang up and began firing like a madman, "DIE YOU BASTARDS." Enraged, John shot again and again, using every firearm he carried. The girl gave him a brief glance and smile. The bad news was that the infected was taking minimal to no damage from the firearms, whereas he was frantically racing around after the girl, although she outran him every time they ran. The girl was effective in diverting the level five, but they were not successful in causing any damage to him. They appeared to be losing energy without making any progress; they were all at their limitations. The girl was in no condition to fight longer, yet she persisted until Aiden approached her and questioned, "That letter you threw? What does it mean?"...

"What?" The girl responded, bewildered. "I didn't leave any kind of note"

Aiden was stunned as he looked at her with astonishment. "What was written on that note?" The girl inquired, her face tense as she glanced at him...

"I don't have it, however".

"In that note, there was a route out from these floors," Aiden said. "There were no pictures, only a riddle." The girl stared at him with a strange yet perplexing expression, "A riddle?"....

"Yup, why are you shocked?" Aiden said as he watched the infected approaching them. "Listen! My friend Millie is the only one who enjoys riddles." As she used her nunckuck to fight the infected, the girl replied. Those multiple shackles made the infected sluggish. "Would you mind giving me the note?" The girl asked as Aiden answered with a mournful face that he didn't have the note with him since he tossed it away. "Then go get it! That might be the only way for us to escape." The girl urged Aiden to pick up the pace.

Aiden ran to the spot where he had thrown the paper, however there was nothing there; the note had vanished. He hastily looked around in the hopes of finding it since it could have flown away. The girl noticed him struggling and ran towards him; the infected noticed these two and, considering that they were far away, opted to attack John and Kyle, who were barely standing on their feet. "Don't worry Anna, we won't hurt you," Nate said, laughing with his team.

Anna was strapped to a wheel chair, her lips were taped shut, and she couldn't move. They all arrived at the building's lab, where Nate painstakingly removed the tape as Anna remained silent in pain.... "What do you want from me?" Anna said, out of breath. "You impress me Anna, there's something exceptional about you," Nate stated as he bent his knee and stared into Anna's eyes. "Who in the world are you, anyway?" Anna shouted as the hunter advanced, but Nate quickly pushed him back. Nate burst out laughing like a lunatic once again. "I am the leader of this building, Kid," he stated....

"What? You," Anna said, disagreeing with Nate on the subject. "I believe I am the person you were seeking to meet, ADRIEN!" Nate said with a solemn grin, "Ha ha- he died a long time ago."....

"So this whole time we were just-" Anna stayed silent and whispered slowly. "Are you trying to say something?" Nate responded by standing up and ordering his guys to confine her in a cell before beginning their experiment. "What! In a cell?!" Anna screamed as she was led away by hunter and thrown in a cell. Nate walked into a different room with his team, leaving Hunter in charge of keeping an eye out for Anna. She was thrown into the cell; she could move and use her hands; she was free but stuck in a large cell; she observed Hunter and began banging on the glass walls, calling him an asshole for throwing her inside.

Hunter slowly began advancing towards other cells in front of Anna, and he quickly exposed each cell by sliding a sheet that had been covering it.

Anna gradually saw the large sheet sliding, and when it hit the ground, the scene stunned her; there were others like Anna, but they were unstable. "There are people just like you," Hunter replied as he returned to Anna. "What? I'm not one of them!" Anna denied it. "These guys are called Human-infected just like us, have you ever heard of human-infected before?" Hunter sighed. "No, I haven't," Anna said, perplexed. Hunter exposed his hand by removing a piece of hand armor; his entire hand was covered with infected bite marks...

"People like us are extremely rare; we do not become infected when they bite us; instead, we just grow stronger," Hunter stated as he wore the hand piece armor back. "What? But- how?" Anna said calmly, she was curious about what was going on, and despite the fact that Hunter had thrown her in the cell, she felt comfortable talking to him....

"The infection, which spreads without the help of a human being, has a miniscule probability of enhancing your body rather than killing you and turning you into one of them," Hunter explained. "We are not going to kill you, but we need to do certain tests or you will die."

Anna was bewildered; she didn't want to accept what Hunter was saying, yet she knew deep down that he was right somehow......

"But what about them and you? You seem to be in good health, yet they-" Anna replied while staring at the other cell where the person was out of control; he was still conscious, trying to speak, something a regular infected cannot do, but his body was gradually decaying on its own, which appeared implausible. "These infections are far more deadly to those who become human-infected, it kills you slowly leading in an extremely painful death, but it can be controlled," hunter responded as he reminded Anna that they would not kill her but rather cure her. "But what about John?" Anna questioned Hunter. "They're like family to me; I can't lose them."

Hunter gave her a melancholy look, stayed silent, and slowly placed the cloth on the cell, while Anna gazed at him with tears in her eyes. "The level five dashed and straight attacked Kyle, he got pushed off, thankfully he wasn't bleeding due to the shackles of the infected, but he definitely was in pain.

The next person was John, "No, no, no!!" The girl yelled as she witnessed Kyle being pushed away, and John is the next victim of the infected. She hurried as fast as she could to John, however it was too late; the infected swung his hand on John, sending him flying, while he was unable to do anything.

The infected attempted striking John again, but this time the girl came and immediately pushed John away.

Nonetheless, the infected attacked, and seeing that they had no option but to die, the girl stepped forward to take the strike, even though she had no idea who she was defending or who John was. John witnessed the infected hand coming down on them, and the girl leaping in between. During this brief moment, John spotted a pink necklace on the girl's neck, which shocked him. John swiftly pushed the girl aside and was about to take the strike when the infected was electrocuted and collapsed to the ground.

The girl and John exchanged glances, and another flashback flashed to John in which he saw himself organizing a party, he attached all the balloons and was set for the perfect celebration for her daughter Sally's birthday. Within a few minutes, everything was ready, and they were all delighted to celebrate Sally's birthday; as shortly as she walked into, she was greeted by all of her school friends, and she joyfully blew out her birthday candles. Mike approached Sally and handed her a small box. "Did you get me a present?" Sally yelled with ecstasy. She leaped in joy and hugged Mike and her father while she opened the box and discovered a beautiful necklace inside.

"Millie?" As she glanced at her friend racing towards her, the girl murmured "What are you doing here?"

Millie was sweating and in a hurry; she believed she had a dreadful nightmare, but she understood deep down that in the post-apocaliptic world, every step you undertake is no less than a nightmare, and the nightmare never stops, whether you sleep or wake up.

Millie yelled again as she noticed the girl submerged in her thoughts. "We have to leave! It's urgent" Millie stated as she told everyone that they are being attacked by a group known as UnMarked. "What? UnMarked?" John expressed his shock, to which Millie said, "The strongest group in the other city." She took out a map, and it was precisely the same as John's. There was an area labeled UnMarked. Aiden and Kyle were astonished to see that the location they were aiming to go was not a location but rather a group of individuals attacking this building.

ELEVEN

The Final War

"We don't have time to discuss right now; follow me to the bunker beneath this building and I'll tell you everything," Millie said as she dashed forward, unlocking a tiny door. Anna remained oblivious to what was happening on outside. "HUNTER! We are being attacked!" Nate yelled as he and his guys burst into the lab. "What? They've arrived!" Hunter responded as he rushed to open Anna's cell, telling her "Stay with us, we are under attack." Anna nodded and began walking behind Hunter, although she still disliked Nate.

On the other side, John and everyone entered a bunker beneath the building, where John's first query was, "Anna! What about her? We must save her."

"She's OK, believe me," the girl said as John gazed at her, "How can, you be sure? The men ahead of us just attacked her" As wrath could be heard in John's voice, he remarked.......

"I know how Hunter is, he won't let anyone injure someone like his type," the girl replied while John was perplexed. "One of his?" he inquired....

"She's human-infected." The girl responded, however Aiden cut her off. "Hence the concept of human-infected is real," he added....

"Yeah, it is" Millie answered "especially her, when a person gets human-infected that person develops ability that is far more superior than any human being but there is just one flaw that they suffer the most slow painful death someone can ever feel."

John was worried about Anna and wanted to find a way to save her, however the girl consoled him by telling that they took her to provide her with the best remedy. "That's absolute bullshit!" John yelled as he stated that the men who tried to kill them couldn't save Anna. He even questioned the girl and Millie questioning why they were trying to help them. The girl stated that they needed to leave this building for whatever reason. "Why?" John questioned them since he found this statement perplexing. "I can't tell you," The girl answered as John persisted again.

The girl stared at Millie, they both took a swift breath, and Millie began to speak, "There used to be another leader of this building, he was killed by Nate, which gave him the power to rule this entire place." "It makes no sense," John responded, perplexed by what Millie was attempting to imply. "Many people were unhappy with the current ruler, so Nate gathered other survivors to revolt with him and attack them if they didn't listen, and the worst happened, the entire city went to war, destroying everything, all the stores, coffee shops, trains, or god knows what." Millie replied with a sorrowful grin as she gazed at the girl. "Unfortunately, Nate won, which resulted in Adrien Hart's death," the girl added as Aiden sank in horror. He shouted over and over, "NO! Shut Up" The girl gave him a disappointed look and tried to convince him that his brother was murdered by none other than Nate himself.

"We don't need to leave this building then," Aiden stated, shocking everyone in the room except John. He agreed with Aiden and requested the girl and Millie to help them in navigating the building.

"We can't because we're under attack!" Millie insisted that they must wait in this bunker for a brief period of time before striking since the UnMarked survivor team is far more strong.

"How long do we have to wait?" John wondered, his adrenaline rushing, as he and Aiden prepared to avenge Adrien Hart's death and Saving Anna's life, even if they are trying to help her. Aiden stared at him and agreed, realizing that John would therefore help him.

Kyle, on the other hand, took a step forward, saying, "You all were right, I might have messed up before, but I think I am ready." John stared at him and nodded, and they all turned to Millie to make the final decision. "If you believe you're ready, I can't stop you, but there are some things we need to take care of," Millie stated as she brought out a precise map of the building, which was much larger than they thought from the exterior. "But there's one thing I don't understand," Kyle said. "You despised Nate, but he let you live with him?"
"Nate used to be an assistant working in a laboratory. before the pandemic, everyone looked at him as if he was nothing but a slave, however what they didn't know was that he was a genius, he often used to screw up things without leaving a trace trying to come up with some I don't know- some sort of chemical or elixir that turn humans like other animals and makes them powerful," the girl stated to Kyle. Millie watched everyone's faces and realized that they were all curious about Nate, and that if they kept telling Nate's story, they would be able to have some time to stay here instead of bursting out like a lunatic and dying.

"You're telling me he's the reason this catastrophe started in the first place?" John questioned; his face muck sweat. The bunker was noticeably overheated. "Many people believe that, but we disagree." Millie said "The laboratory in which he had worked was not the same as we had seen in the broadcast or media." "So you still believe in news?" In disbelief and wrath, John said "Well, what else do we have to believe in?" Millie said, flinging her hands in the air. "Damn it, John, we need to go out, whatever Nate did, he has to pay the price for it," Aiden snarled, interrupting Millie and getting up in rage. Millie knew they weren't going to halt them at this point, so she calmly pointed to the building's map and instructed them they had to go by the emergency exit from this bunker. Aiden urged Millie to hand him the map and that he would take care of everything from here.

Millie was skeptical at first, but she understood this was necessary, thus she handed them the map and led them to the door. They all went over. "And how about you two?" As he noticed them not passing through the door, John inquired......

"We'll catch you up from the other side, although there are some things to take care of first," Millie replied, gazing at her pal.

Aiden smiled at them and began moving out; John pulled Kyle up and they were now inside an empty basement. Aiden was enraged, whilst John was calm and chilly. The girl and Millie, on the other hand, hastily opened their main entrance and bolted as fast as they could; their entire building was on blaze, signifying that the onslaught had already begun. "MILLIE! WHAT ON EARTH ARE YOU DOING THERE?" Hunter shouted as he forced them to follow Nate and many others ahead of him.

They first halted and began withdrawing, however when they recognized Anna among them, their minds were altered, and they resolved to watch after her until John and everyone showed up. "Hey! Anna"

The girl approached her quickly since they didn't had time. Anna took a short glance at them and questioned, "Where is everyone else?"...

"They'll be here soon, just hang on," the girl stated as they established visual contact with Nate. He was drenched in blood, carrying a large gun, while he gazed at Millie and the girl. "Are you either fine or hurt?" He stated as he kept holding himself up while it became apparent that he had a fractured leg. "Don't tell me they're all alone by themselves," Anna said in horror and wrath as she looked at them.......

"They'll be here soon, don't worry about it." The girl remarked as she saw Anna walk away from everyone else, enraged.

Hunter gradually spotted two of the intruders in front of him preparing to attack, thus he crept forward quickly and stealthily; he wasn't carrying a gun; however, he did keep one in his backpack.

Once he got closer towards one of them, a survivor from the back aimed a gun at him. "Where do you think you're going?" He stated while pointing his rifle firmly. Hunter heard him, the survivor was behind him, yet Hunter didn't care, he quickly rose up while the other two survivors arrived, leaving it three against one. Hunter stood there with a slight grin on his face, all three intruders surrounding him.

Hunter walked slowly as the attackers fired at him. He collapsed to the ground, believing that they had killed Hunter, The three intruders began moving and laughing hysterically, however Hunter abruptly rose up.

The three survivors were astounded to see Hunter still standing, and the gunshot traces had vanished. "Who the hell are you?" The survivor inquired as he began to sweat and his pulse skipped a beat. Hunter smiled creepily before slaughtering all three survivors in a matter of seconds. Anna was still sprinting, while the girl hollered at Nate, questioning why he wasn't stopping her. Nate replied, "The entire building has already been attacked, we can't leave, and there are no survivors left, therefore the only place she will remain alive is with us, so wait, she will comeback."

The girl and Millie were eager; therefore, they began rushing as well. Within several seconds, the hunter returned, claiming that he had cleared the way and that they could all proceed, including Nate and the other survivors. Hunter observed Anna had left and asked Nate what happened to her....

"She ran away, though she'll come back, we should keep moving," Nate answered while he slowly stepped ahead. "No Nate, she's too dangerous to be left alone, I am not going anywhere till she returns," Hunter replied as Nate grew infuriated. Hunter was not pleased. Hunter's eyes became crimson red as he gazed at Nate, however Nate wasn't bothered. Hunter ultimately embraced Nate and began moving, turning back one last time hoping to see Anna running back, but she didn't.

Anna went straight back inside the laboratory since it was closer towards the floor where she witnessed a level five infected running violently with rage, yet nobody was there. She returned but was shortly approached by the girl and Millie. "What the heck, Anna? Come with us. "Millie urged as she drew her away, however Anna was not pleased. She pushed her back and refused to come. "What are they even worth to you?" Millie yelled in fury as she was hurt when Anna shoved her.

Anna was outraged to hear that; thus, she quickly rose up. They all observed Anna's dark crimson eyes, and they concluded that Anna had the power of the human-infected.

Hunter instantly sensed something and began moving; Nate was enraged, nevertheless he eventually went with him. "They mean a lot to me," Anna growled. The girl gently grasped Anna's hand in hers and spoke her her tale. She stated that she, too, had lost both of her parents, which made Anna slightly less upset. She looked at her and stated that John is the last person she can rely upon and that she doesn't want to lose him...

"Don't worry, we'll help you," the girl said as she held her hands while Anna's eyes returned to normal. "But who is John?" Millie inquired from behind..."John Baker," Anna replied as she turned to face her. As she realized who John was, the girl's hand started trembling.......

"Hey, are you all right?" Anna questioned her as she noticed she was trembling. But before they did anything, Hunter arrived at the place, followed by Nate. "What the hell is going on?" hunter wondered as he cautioned everyone about the dangers of roaming in this area. A booming blast signaled that the onslaught was in full swing. The floor under them began to fall, and they all fled to the lab to rescue themselves, but the building was on the verge of collapsing at any moment.

The entire group of attackers began flooding inside, eventually being engaged in the struggle with the level five, however Nate and Hunter realized that the level five wouldn't be able to bear much longer, thus he swiftly ordered everyone to move inside and find a way to exit. They all rushed inside; however, it was too late because all the attackers began circling him.

Hunter instantly began killing each of the attackers he spotted, but because of the sheer number of attackers, he was becoming sluggish. Anna joined the fight and battled them. Nate gunned down all of the attackers, yet they nevertheless managed to find a method to fire at them.

The fight had begun, and the attackers have nearly taken over the entire building. John, Aiden, and Kyle were revisiting the building's floors. There were still several attackers around in front of them. They stealthily eliminated several of the attackers and continued advancing, unaware that they had already been outnumbered by the UnMarked.

They persisted, though. "Let's hope we find Nate before these attackers do," Aiden remarked upon noticing another note on the floor, however before he had a chance to act on it, he was attacked from behind by one of the attackers. Aiden was fortunate that he survived since the bullet wasn't close to him. Kyle and John began firing; however, they were forced to withdraw.

They crouched behind a wall, their hearts thumping. Aiden noticed an inconspicuous gap within the ceiling and hurriedly told everyone to follow him through, so they all walked through there and discovered a blazing hall full with chained infected. It was a long hall with infected guarding every step they took. "This looks insane," Kyle said, peering around. The infected were handless, yet they could still bite and infect anyone. While seeking for a way out, John saw something in the center that was positioned just like a trophy when you go through this massive horde of infected.

He swiftly tapped Aiden on the shoulder and showed out the object in the center.

"Do you see what that is?" While Aiden and Kyle glanced at the object, john replied.

"How do we get there?" Kyle pondered, adding that eradicating all of the infected would be an eternity. "These infected are chained, you idiot, we don't have to kill every one of them," John replied, still in astonishment and curious about the mystery of the object in the middle....

"Looks like we'll have to find out for ourselves," Aiden muttered as he readied to slay the infected with a knife, while Kyle pulled out his rifle. "What are you up to?" As John said, they couldn't fire weapons since the attackers may hear them and follow them in, however the attackers had already discovered the opening in the ceiling and were attempting to penetrate it.

John with everybody were ready to execute the infected until they heard a noise coming out of that precise gap; they realized they were being pursued by the attackers and had to devise a plan to flee. Aiden suggested that since they couldn't really see an exit, they should try to go and hide among the infected since the attackers would have a great difficulty seeing and killing all of the infected. The three wasted no time and quickly rushed to merge with the infected, however it was perilous because the infected could still bite and turn them into one of them. Aiden and John took the narrow path, but Kyle had different intentions; he crouched behind a big infected that was barely moving and covered much of the area; his aim was to exterminate all of the attackers. John spotted Kyle and tried to call him; however, he couldn't yell or shout as a result of the attackers.......

"Why is Kyle acting like an idiot?" John said softly to Aiden as they approached the center.

The attackers ended up breaking through the gap and immediately aimed the rifle toward them, uncovering all the infected shackled and, fortunately, no glimpse of John, Aiden, or Kyle. The attackers understood that this was the sole place the three of them could have gone. The attackers didn't depart right away, instead threw grenades into the massive horde, and given that the infected were shackled, they couldn't flee and went insane attempting to unchain themselves.

Kyle was shoved by the large infected, and as a consequence, he collapsed to the ground as well as the infected piled on him, suffocating him. The attackers began wandering around and came close to Kyle; they observed the fat infected and were quickly disguised by it; fortunately, Kyle was not in their sights. "What is that?" the attacker inquired to his teammate. "What, where?" his buddy said, puzzled. "In the middle," the attacker answered, captivated by the fact that the object in the middle was coated in glass and had something sparkling inside of it. However, it was still obstructed by the running infected.

Aiden observed a lumber on the ground however as he glanced up he realized that the object in the center was glassed and within there was a golden vase which was entirely sealed and on the glass there was a wooden plank labeled as "ADRIEN HART."

Aiden was taken aback as he discovered it was his brother's ashes which had been deposited there by all the survivors who were with Adrien in order for him to stay as their leader. John became aware of this and turned to face Aiden. "Does that mean-"

"All of the infected that were shackled were with Adrien," Aiden stated. "It appears Nate committed all of this because they elected Adrien as their leader."

Aiden was enraged but also touched by seeing his brother's ashes, thus he chose to carry the vase with him. The attackers, however, were still on the lookout for what was within that glass....

"But still, Aiden How are we supposed to cope with them?" As Aiden proposed an idea, John inquired. John was apprehensive at first, but he understood that it was the sole option. Aiden pointed his rifle towards the attacker's head and prepared to pull the trigger. He continued to sweat as his heart raced, while he hallucinated his brother begging, "Help me, brother, please." Aiden began to shake, but he controlled himself. John observed this and mumbled to Aiden, "Keep focused, now isn't the time." Aiden comprehended and adjusted his aim, as John drew his firearm and prepared to shoot them.

"In memory of Adrien"

As the bullet struck, the entire group of attackers in the hall perished at the exact same instant. "What the Hell?" John exclaimed as he sprang up in disbelief, while Aiden remained silent but mystified. Kyle eventually managed to shove the fat dead infected off him and discovered that all of the attackers have nearly died.

They were all completely unaware of what had just occurred. The entire hall was empty, all the infected were dead, and no attackers were around.

They all gathered there quietly for a couple of moments until, "Dad," the girl said as John spun around in horror, bleeding due to the grenades, yet he was alive and his body was functioning......

"S- Sa- Sally?" While John gazed at his daughter, who was wearing the very same necklace as the girl who struggled to save John from the level five infected, it became clear that the girl with them was in fact ***John's daughter "Sally."***

TWELVE

Dead But Alive

John's gun dropped to the ground as he raced to grab her. They both ran to each other, tears streaming down their faces. They were overjoyed to finally meet each other and were about to hold each other when a rifle was fired out of the blue. The gunshot was fired by a barely conscious attacker, and it struck John in the back. The entire place went dark. Sally seemed to have the sensation that everything was occurring in slow motion as she watched John slam to the ground. Surprisingly, John discovered he was not in agony or bleeding. Everyone was stunned when John turned around and found that Anna had caught the bullet.

John was heartbroken and couldn't believe what he had witnessed. "NO!" he cried as he raced to get her. Anna was unresponsive until, all of a sudden,

"Oh boy, what do we have here?" Nate said, laughing hysterically. Aiden swiftly shielded John by aiming his rifle at Nate, however Nate was immediately shielded by the hunter at his side. John held Anna in one arm while pointing at the hunter with the other. "This is not the time to have fun! She's just a kid, and we're in need of your aid, you jerks!" John yelled in agony.

"First of all, that's extremely bold of you, second of all, she's a human-infected, she can't die with such a bullet regardless of whether it was shot in her skull," Nate mocked John and his crew.

John remained enraged, and everything he said was fueled by rage and sorrow....

"You're going to pay for everything." Aiden screamed as he began to pull the trigger but instead was halted by Sierra from behind. "In battle, you must always look around you," Sierra stated as she positioned her rifle on Aiden's head. Kyle added as he pointed his rifle towards Sierra's back, "I could say the same thing." Sierra was taken aback, and Aiden flashed a little smirk, which Nate caught afterwards.

"Enough of this melodrama, let's finish them, Hunter," Nate yelled, but was suddenly blocked by Millie and Sally in front of them. "You too?" Nate acknowledged his amazement at seeing one of them turn against him. "You are the reason Adrien died, you are the reason my father was going to die, YOU ARE THE REASON MIKE IS DEADDD!" Everyone in the hallway, excluding Nate and Hunter, was horrified as Sally blurted out the truth....

"Sally, what are you talking about?" In a state of awe and rage, John replied

"Everything was been planned, DAD! When Nate found the existence of Aiden upon killing Adrien, he sent men to look for him in order to kill him since he knew Aiden will indeed seek out him since he killed his brother, and he even knew that the sole human who could kill him was Aiden, so he ordered each and every person to kill and whomever who knew Aiden, which is why you were all chased by the infected everywhere you went.

Nate released all the infected to stop you even when you were approaching this building, and he's the reason I lost my brother and was about to lose MY DAD." Sally yelled as he yanked the rifle from Aiden's hands and fired directly at Nate, miraculously wounding him in the chest.

The final battle had already begun.

Hunter grew outraged and raced to Sally, striking her hard and causing her to collapse on the ground; fortunately, Millie caught her; Sally wasn't bleeding but was left with a slight scar. Sierra rushed to Nate, believing that Hunter would easily take care of everyone by himself.

Hunter raced to Aiden and punched him repeatedly, making Aiden show weakness and causing him to bleed. Hunter swiftly moved to John, just as he was about to deliver a punch, his blow was promptly intercepted, which astonished Hunter since it was practically impossible to catch a punch from a human-infected, and it was Anna. "No, Hunter, I'm not going to let you touch him," Anna said as Hunter attempted to persuade her by stating, "You should come with me, Anna; I can teach you and strengthen you."

"NO! Leave this place "Anna yelled such as she pushed hunter with all her might. Hunter was flung away, while John shot him, but it didn't help. "How do we defeat a human-infected, Anna?" Once John understood Hunter was speaking the truth about bullets not working on human-infected, he queried.

Sierra stepped within the nearest undamaged part of the building and placed Nate down. Nate glanced at her carefully and withdrew a key from his pocket and handed it to Sierra.

"This contains the capacity to annihilate the whole city, go to the control panel it's on seventh floor, the door's already open, enter through it and put this key on the red region right in middle and push it as it's the only choice we have to survive these attackers. Sierra nodded to Nate and dashed up the steps, clutching the key in her fingers. "Sierra! Take my rifle, you need it more than I do," Nate remarked

Nate passed the rifle after seeing Sierra rushing up the stairs; he glanced around and realized nobody was around, therefore he took a bottle labeled ***southern lab chem***, opened the top quickly, and drank the entire contents. Nothing occurred for a few seconds; however, Nate soon began to experience severe agony and uncontrolled movement. Hunter was fighting Anna, who was putting up a good battle until Hunter decided to give it his all. Anna was shoved by the hunter and crashed to the ground; John attempted to intervene but was no match for the hunter. "You can't kill me," Hunter exclaimed as he began to go insane. Suddenly, From behind, a slow, gravelly voice said, "HUNTER." Everyone in the room looked around while Hunter laughed uncontrollably. Standing behind them, they discovered something that stunned everyone in the room.

"Nate-" Hunter grinned once again. "You found the Southern lab."

Nate had completely transformed, he was much larger than before, that he had turned into a level five human-infected. "Are human-infected people have levels?" Kyle mused, standing there afraid yet determined. "They do," Hunter responded, "so now we can govern this city together, with no one to stop us."

Nate laughed uproariously at Hunter as Hunter became perplexed, then his smile faded....

"What does it mean?" Hunter inquired, his face solemn and his gaze fixed on Nate's. "Oh, no, we certainly can, but- ***Prove me***"....

"We have two traitors in this room, I need you to kill them," Nate remarked, motioning Hunter to kill Sally and Millie. Hunter turned to face them, and everyone gazed at him as he carefully withdrew a gun from his rucksack, reloaded it, and was getting ready to shoot. Nate smiled at Hunter while he cautiously positioned his rifle; everyone looked at him in dread, and some stood helpless. Hunter quickly altered the rifle position at the last second and shot Nate instead of Sally and Millie.......

"What the hell Hunter?" Nate yelled in agony, as everyone was stunned to witness Hunter shooting one of their own. Nate had no scars; however, it was agonizing since it was fired in a specific location. "Listen to me, level five may be the toughest, but they have one fatal flaw, straight in their heart, which is the only vulnerable location for an infected." Hunter hurriedly ordered everyone to prepare to face Nate. Sierra was headed towards the fifth-floor stairs when she was intercepted by two of the attackers who appeared to be moving through. "Hey, stop right there," the attackers yelled as Sierra ran for the stairs. She began racing up the flights of stairs while the two survivors pursued her.

Sierra outran them but was stopped when she observed something weird in front of her, she was trapped, as she spotted some infection grasping her leg. A guy arrived without a trace and grabbed Sierra tightly.

"Where is Nate?" enquired the guy in a black suit, who resembled an agent and had a hat, black glasses, as well as a black tie. "Why- Who?" Sierra uttered, choking from the guy's grasp on her neck.

"Don't act, or you'll all die," the guy replied slowly, while gazing down at the floor and immediately beginning deviating, leaving Sierra alone. She was perplexed when she noticed the infection grabbing her began following the guy. "Who the heck is he?" Sierra stated as she peered up and noticed one of his hands twisting and turning red. "Can he be a human-infect- never mind, I need to focus on my plan," Sierra remarked as she dashed for the sixth floor.

She was instantaneously met with hordes of infected in front of her; she observed them and began running in the opposite way, "Damn it, dang it." Yet, to her amazement, the infected simply passed her, following the very same way the guy took after abandoning Sierra. She observed that all of the infected in front of her were strolling by her without attacking her. She soon made her way to the sixth floor and found herself just one floor away from razing the whole city.

Nate on the other hand, was enraged and began mumbling wacky things while laughing hysterically. Everyone had some form of vulnerability, and Hunter had taken the lead, guarding everyone, even though he knew that everyone would die under him.

The boulder's size was massive, capable of obliterating a significant portion of the people in the room. Consequently, everyone instinctively lowered their gaze, apprehensively anticipating the worst. However, Hunter remained standing, resolute and determined to employ every ounce of his strength to prevent the disaster from unfolding.

Suddenly, just as the massive boulder was about to strike them, it came to an abrupt stop. John tentatively opened his eyes and was surprised to see the colossal rock motionless right in front of him. "What the heck just happened?" Nate exclaimed in confusion.

The rest of the people in the room were equally bewildered, unsure of what had just occurred to prevent the boulder from crushing them. "Take a look at the bottom of the boulder; it's the infection," Anna stated, pointing out the cause of the interruption. As they all looked down, they noticed that the infection had somehow managed to halt the attack mid-way. Nate disregarded the situation and started advancing towards them on his own, but everyone else remained frozen in place, avoiding eye contact with the dangerous boulder.... "If this plan fails, I can still take you out by myself," Nate threatened as he made his way towards Sally and Millie first. However, Hunter quickly intervened and jumped in between them, determined to prevent any harm from coming to his friends. "NO, you will not move from here," Hunter declared sternly, blocking Nate's path and refusing to let him continue any further..."Get out of my way, Hunter, or you'll die with them!" Nate barked, his expression hard and unyielding.

Hunter knew that Nate wasn't messing around anymore, but neither was he. "Make me, Nate. If that's what it takes to save them," Hunter responded, looking at Sally and Millie while murmuring a quick "sorry" to them. Nate didn't utter a single word, instead choosing to attempt to punch Hunter.

However, to everyone's surprise, his hand was abruptly halted mid-air, despite no one holding or restraining him.

"Did you do that, Hunter?" Kyle asked from behind, wondering if there was an alternative way to defeat Nate. Hunter stood motionless, sweat beading on his forehead as his heart raced in his chest. "Tell me, Hunter, was it you?" Kyle shouted, while Nate struggled to free himself. "Are you okay, Hunter?" Millie asked anxiously from behind, concerned for his well-being.

Suddenly, slow footsteps could be heard, and to everyone's surprise, the mysterious man that Sierra had encountered earlier finally appeared before them.

It became evident that he was the reason why Nate was immobilized and couldn't move. As Nate attempted to struggle and move around, he finally caught a glimpse of the man's black appearance... "Who are you?" Nate demanded to know, intrigued by the stranger's sudden arrival. The man slowly took off his hat and began to reach for his glasses, but then paused. "Not this easily. You have to kill me," he stated sternly. "And all of you- Hunter, Sally, and Millie- I know who you all are, and-"

However, the man's words trailed off as he caught sight of Aiden, who was badly wounded. Letting out a heavy sigh, he then suggested that they all leave the area, warning them that the city was about to be destroyed, and the fight against the human-infected would be deadly for ordinary humans.

Hunter immediately complied with the man's suggestion, knowing that Sierra had left the area due to the possibility of Nate ordering her to blow up the city. He also realized that it was essential for the safety of Sally, Millie, and everyone else to evacuate the area. Without hesitation, Hunter quickly grabbed Sally and Millie's hands and urged everyone to follow him. "Anna, go get John, Aiden, and Kyle. Hurry!" he shouted, his voice echoing through the room as they made their way out. "No, you cannot leave! I will kill you!" Nate yelled as he struggled to break free from his restraints.

As he was about to attack, the mysterious man stopped him once again, but this time it was clear that he was struggling to hold Nate back. "You have to fight me now!" The man demanded, causing Nate to turn around and face him, allowing Hunter and the others to make their escape......

"You have a problem, I see," Nate taunted as he broke free once more and punched the man, causing his glasses to crack.

However, the man quickly stood up and ordered his men to attack. In just seconds, the room was filled with people attacking Nate....

"You really think these humans with their guns can kill me?" Nate laughed as he moved with incredible speed, killing his attackers one by one....

"You might think this is stupid, but I only used this to distract you," the man said, causing Nate to become perplexed. He looked around and realized that the man was no longer in sight. "Sometimes you forget that I am also a human-infected," the man stated, suddenly appearing out of nowhere and delivering a powerful punch to Nate's chest, weakening his defenses and bringing him one step closer to his demise.

Hunter and the others had to think quickly as they found themselves trapped on the first floor of the building. The attackers had destroyed the stairs, blocking their escape route. In a moment of quick thinking, Hunter and Anna jumped down to assess if the route was safe for the rest of the group.

Once everyone had made it down to the first floor, they realized that the entire bottom of the building was flooded, and the only way out was through a canal that they had previously entered through. Sally was the first to speak up, asking Hunter where they should go next. Hunter quickly responded, stating that there was only one option - they had to jump. Kyle, however, was hesitant, arguing that the height was too great and it would not be safe to make the jump. Despite Kyle's concerns, Hunter stood firm and insisted that they had no other choice but to take the leap.

With Hunter leading the way, they all prepared themselves to jump down to the canal below.

They knew the risk involved, but it was the only way to escape the dangerous situation they found themselves in. As they took a deep breath and prepared to jump, they all hoped for a safe landing. Anna spoke up, affirming Kyle that it would be safe for them to jump. She explained that Hunter and she would create an easy way to jump from the lowest angle possible. Hunter chimed in, pointing out a covered canal that would provide them with protection from the blast. He couldn't guarantee their survival, but it was their best shot at making it out alive. Despite their skepticism, the group knew they had no other choice.

John reminded them that they were already dead if it weren't for Hunter's help, so they had to take this chance. Sally nodded, her confidence shining through her expression. Hunter wasted no time and grabbed Sally and Millie, jumping into the canal in an instant. The water's flow was strong, causing them to be thrown about like rag dolls. They were unable to swim, but eventually found themselves in the flow of the water. Kyle expressed his doubts, saying that it looked like a suicide plan. Anna was irritated by his comments and pushed him into the stream.

She then grabbed John's and Aiden's hands, smiling, and jumped into the canal with them. The group was now in the water, unsure of what lay ahead, but united in their determination to survive.

Nate, on the other hand, was consistently getting nailed by the guy until he managed to foresee all the places the guy was approaching from and immediately attacked on an unexpected side, causing the guy to drift away from Nate.

The guy simply stood up to realize that this approach would just not work anymore, so he roared at Nate, "Let's have a fair battle, hand to hand like real men!" Nate was experiencing something unordinary at this point, he was amazingly turning into an infected. The guy started to notice this, beginning to realize that hand to hand was the sole way he could kill Nate as his chest was already damaged and all he required was a solitary big punch with all of his strength to finish him.

Sierra arrived on the seventh floor and started to investigate what Nate was referring to; she noticed multiple slots into which she inserted the key and began determining the correct location by testing them individually. Nate didn't hesitate and accepted the hand-to-hand duel. The guy commanded his left men to back off, while they were both set. The guy remained there waiting for Nate to strike, however Nate shared the same idea; they both stood there frozen. "Are you going to fight or what?" the guy questioned...

"I could ask the same question," Nate remarked with a stern smile.

The guy gradually approached him as Nate did the very same, they both drew closer and punched one another in the face, their strengths were equal however the guy had the edge, they both swung yet again but this time Nate opted to block and flanking maneuver the guy. The guy was dazed and was struck in the chest, shattering his ribs, though since he's human-infected, he was still capable of fighting, although in agony.

John and everyone gathered into the canal and sat down, either dying or staying alive. Sally softly held John for assurance; John embraced her as well and discovered Anna sitting alone with her eyes closed, weeping silently; John carefully took her and reassured both of them, "All will be well, trust me."

The guy and Nate went mad fighting each other, the hand-to-hand battle was growing increasingly strong, the construction around them started crumbling, they continued going unless they both became weary, however it wasn't the end, they both remained nine feet apart gazing dead into each other's eyes.

Sierra, on the other hand, sent several random lights and automated systems as she trawled for the right place, but she suddenly noticed a red signal and immediately learned that this was the precise one that Nate was referring to;

She quickly positioned the key and turned it around to the other side as the entire lab shuttered and broadcasted only one thing. *10- 9- 8* "So it's a countdown," Sierra said as she scanned a little warning beside where she had inserted the key that stated that this device ought to only be activated during a catastrophe since it would wipe out the whole city except this building. Sierra didn't have much of a thought, nevertheless it was too late to change anything. The guy and Nate both raced toward each other with their hands out, adequately prepared to punch each other, they were just inches away from hitting each other when the guy suddenly stopped Nate by using the infection and smacked him in the heart. As soon as his hand contacted Nate's heart, the countdown ended, and the city's buildings began to explode individually within a split second.

The explosion was so loud that nobody was able to take it; even the human-infected were struggling; the entire building seemed to have no explosion however was already weak due to the attacks, resulting in collapsing; everything was tumbling; it seemed like witnessing the end of the world yet again.

Thirty minutes had elapsed and everyone in the canal had collapsed and were laying; nobody seemed to be moving at first, but as time passed, John abruptly regained consciousness as his ears still rang yet he was still in agony;

Fortunately, he had lived, and he glanced around while his eyes were tainted. "Sally? Anna?" John yelled as he attempted to rouse everyone.

They cautiously stood up by themselves. Sally awoke alongside them and was overjoyed to find John standing right in front of her; she roused herself and enthusiastically embraced John. Hunter slowly arose and saw John and Sally together, he smiled slightly and began taking care of the remainder of the crew, nobody had died although they were severely injured, once everyone had regained their right state of mind, They all eventually exited the canal and observed that everything had been reduced to ashes, many of which were still burning.

Hunter stared at the building and watched the entire structure collapse into the ground; John discovered the guy who was trapped and severely harmed, his body bleeding profusely because of an enormous rod stabbed through his chest; they all quickly approached him and tried to talk to him. The guy was first unconscious, but then he gradually popped his eyes open. "Hello, are you okay, wait, help me get him out, HURRY," Hunter yelled as he employed every inch of his left might to drag him out, but was immediately halted by the man.

It was the same person who was disguised entirely in black and looked to be an agent; he was severely injured and was gasping his last breaths. "NO, stop, let me be this way, my job here is done." he remarked,

"What Job" John asked as the guy glanced at him "sit down." The person replied, "Killing Nate, My job is over."

"BUT- Who are you, and how did you find out about this?" John inquired as the man offered a little giggle before responding saying he knew Nate was destined to get human-infected, which was the reason he was with Sierra in the first place.... "What about SIERRA?!" John asked, and the guy responded that he had no idea....

"But who are you?" Kyle inquired as the man gently removed his shattered glasses and said,

""I AM ADRIEN HART""

www.ingramcontent.com/pod-product-compliance
Lightning Source LLC
LaVergne TN
LVHW061611070526
838199LV00078B/7240